PRAISE FOR *THE PHOTO HUSTLE*

"I trust Karen's judgment on everything she posts and puts out into the world because she has the experience to back it all up. She's a pillar in the photography industry, and her voice needs to be heard, especially during a time when the industry is calling for more people who know what they are talking about, all while championing the photographers who are creating the content that keeps our industry going. I have read her book, and it's incredibly valuable, eloquently written, and full of passion and heart."
—Kelly Elaine Garthwaite, founder of Hey Y'all!

"Karen's book *The Photo Hustle* is so necessary in the photographer hiring community. She has the exact experience to write such a guide for photographers at any career level in life. I am excited to share her book with the photo community. It is so very needed. I constantly come across photographers who know nothing about the photo business and how to negotiate properly, etc. It's wonderful to have Karen's book to suggest to them, since I haven't seen anything else like it out there. I'm in extreme support of this book."
—Anna Goldwater Alexander, director of photography at *WIRED*

"With over fifteen years of experience in the brand photography industry, Karen Williams possesses a profound depth of knowledge, but what sets her apart is her dedication to demystifying the industry, an arena often perceived as impenetrable. As the CEO and creator of Black Visual Queen, Karen has established herself as a vanguard, tirelessly working to bring diversity and opportunity to the field. Her book is a beacon for any aspiring photographer looking to break into the industry, offering not just hope but practical, actionable strategies that have been proven to work."
—Rob Haggart, A Photo Editor

"Karen Williams is a force within the photography industry, and this book is a beacon of insight and inspiration. Having witnessed her profound expertise and compassionate mentorship firsthand, I am thrilled to offer my support for her work and wholeheartedly endorse Karen's invaluable contribution to our field. I have no doubt that this book will resonate profoundly within the photography and creative communities."

—**Christopher Kern**, program lead and associate professor of photography at California Baptist University

"Karen Williams has an exceptional eye and is a great connector between creative talent and hiring professionals in the photography industry. Particularly in our current visual landscape with so many new platforms and business models rapidly evolving, her perspective will be a very valuable resource for anyone looking for a voice of reason amid the noise!"

—**Ash Barhamand**, visual media director at *The Hollywood Reporter*

"I'm thrilled for the moment when Karen Williams's book *The Photo Hustle* makes its debut to the world. With Karen's extensive experience in the photography industry, her insights hold immeasurable value. Karen has also evolved into a dedicated educator and a champion for photographers, enriching the community through her wealth of knowledge and passion. She will bring her invaluable expertise to the pages of this book."

—**Tracy Woods**, director of photography at The Luupe, creative producer, consultant, and artist

"*The Photo Hustle* is a vital guide for photographers eager to navigate the rapidly evolving industry with authenticity and confidence. What sets this book apart is Karen's unique combination of firsthand experience, deep industry insight, and a genuine commitment to empowering photographers. Her clear, actionable advice on everything from brand versus editorial photography to self-promotion strategies offers both proven tactics and valuable personal wisdom. This book is a must-have for anyone serious about mastering the business and art of photography."

—**Toby Kaufmann**, creative director

THE PHOTO HUSTLE

THE PHOTO HUSTLE

An Insider Guide on How to Book Clients, Get Paid, and Master the Business of Photography

Karen Williams

Copyright © 2025 by Karen Williams.
Published by Black Visual Queen

Cover Design: Karen Williams & Michelle Alynn Clement.
Layout, Design & Illustrations: Michelle Alynn Clement / https://www.michellealynn.com/
Cover Photography: Gabriela Hasbun / https://www.gabrielahasbun.com/
Cover Model: Yasmina Mattison Sudan / https://www.yasminamattisonsudan.com/

For permission requests, please contact the author at:
www.blackvisualqueen.com
Karen@blackvisualqueen.com

For special orders, quantity sales, course adoptions and corporate sales, please email the author at karen@blackvisualqueen.com.
For trade and wholesale sales, please contact Ingram Publisher Services at customer.service@ingramcontent.com or +1.800.509.4887.

The Photo Hustle: An Insider Guide on How to Book Clients, Get Paid, and Master the Business of Photography

Library of Congress Control Number: 2025924065

ISBN: (p) 979-8-9939046-0-3 (e) 979-8-9939046-2-7

BISAC category code: PHO003000 PHOTOGRAPHY / Business Aspects

The content provided in this book is for entertainment and educational purposes only. It is not intended to provide legal, financial, business, or career advice. It should not be used as a substitute for professional counsel or advice from a financial advisor, legal counsel, or business coach. The author and publisher are not responsible for any errors or omissions, or for any outcomes resulting from the use of this information, despite every effort to ensure its accuracy and reliability.

The author and publisher do not permit or make any representations regarding the use or the results of the use of the materials in this book in terms of their correctness, accuracy, reliability, or otherwise. The author and publisher are not liable to any party for any direct, indirect, punitive, special, incidental, or consequential damages that may or may not arise from the use of this book. This book is provided to the reader "as is" without warranty.

Please use your own discretion and consult with legal, financial, or career professionals who can provide tailored advice to your specific situation before making decisions based on this book. The strategies, tips, and tools in this book support your goals, but success is not guaranteed. Your success greatly depends on your amount of motivation, effort, commitment, and follow-through.

To my mom.

My favorite photo assistant, who always
brought me the premium luster paper.

TABLE OF CONTENTS

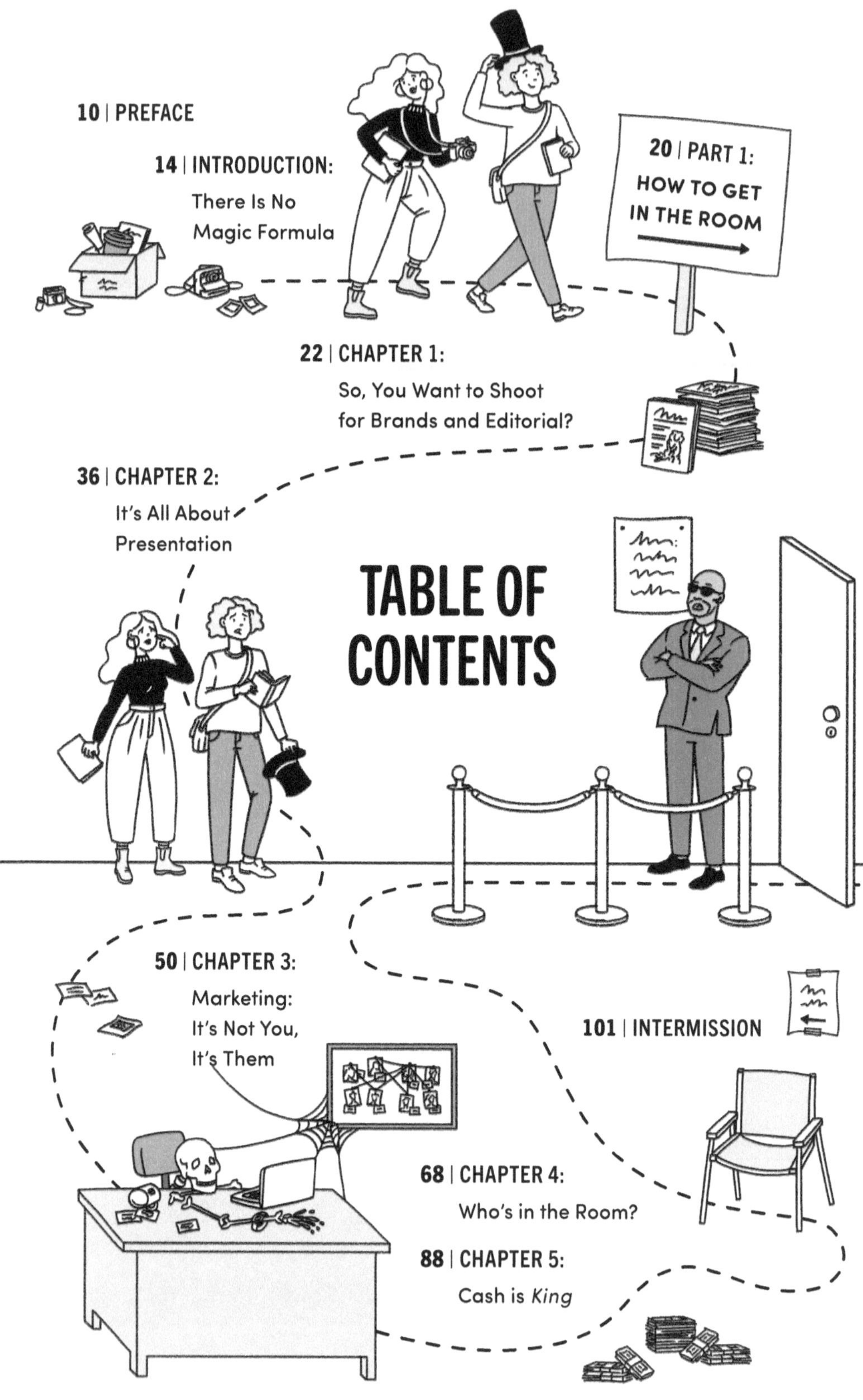

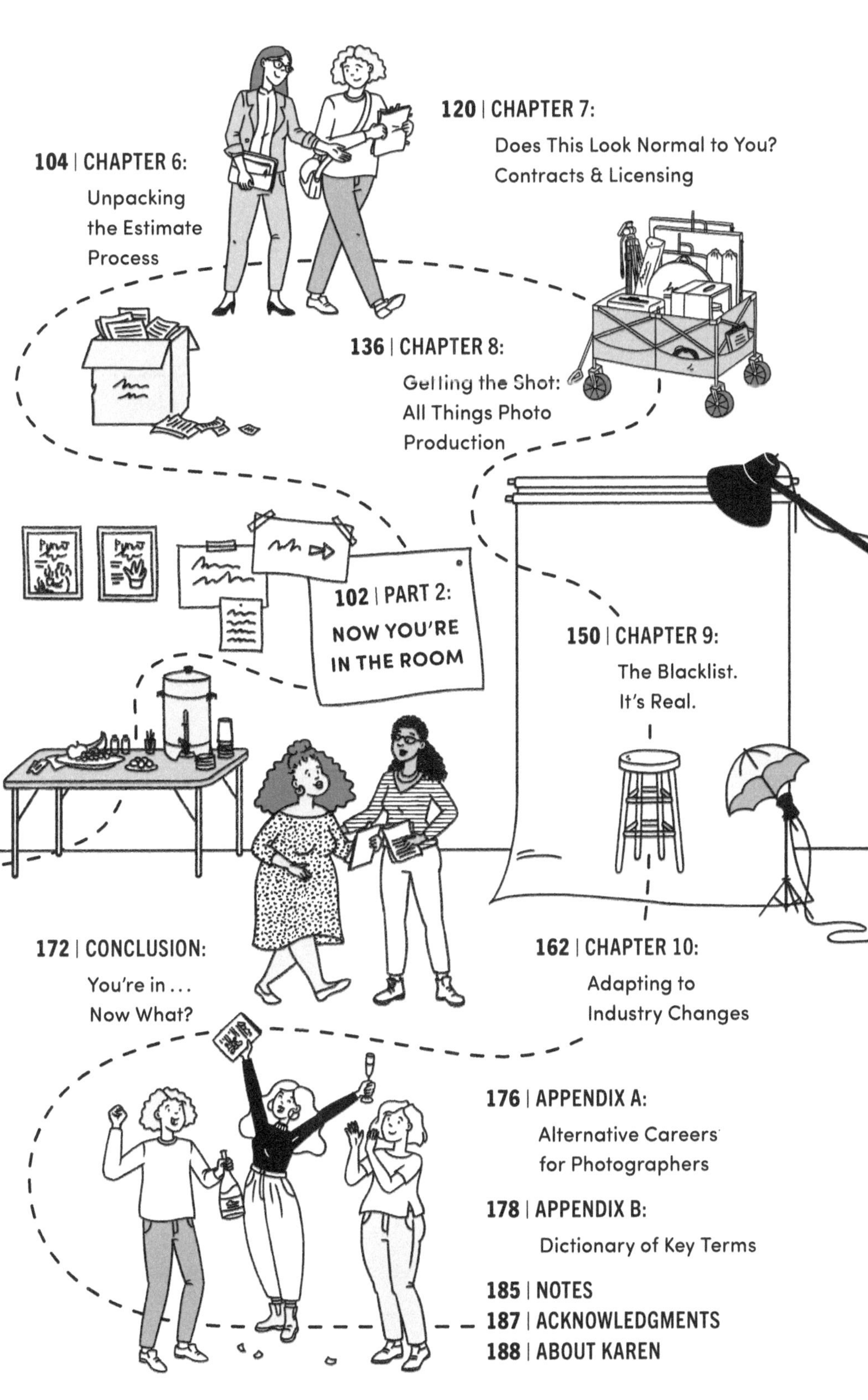

PREFACE

This book is my love letter to the art of photography and to people like you who strive to keep it alive—to make the world a more beautiful place.

My passion for photography was born out of curiosity and my dad's willingness to teach me how to use the family camera. Back then, my interest in photography was simple: I wanted to take the perfect photo. But if I'm honest, I didn't realize there was so much more to taking the "perfect photo" than just making sure it wasn't blurry. I knew nothing about composition, exposure, or lighting techniques—I just knew I liked the act of taking photos. It wasn't until my first real photography course in high school that my love for the art was solidified. I spent countless hours in my high school's janitor-closet-turned-darkroom, learning the ins and outs of developing, exposing, and fixing. I was hooked. From then on, I knew I wanted to be a professional photographer.

There's a common saying that goes something like, "You can't be what you can't see." As a Black woman in America pursuing a career in an industry mostly run by older white men, I needed to see it. Enter Gordon Parks. Parks used his "camera as a weapon against poverty, against racism, and all sorts of social wrongs"[1] to combat the social injustices of his day. Photography can be a force for change.

"When you're forced to look at it, you can't deny it."

—BLACK VISUAL QUEEN

A single image has the power to spark a movement, bring awareness, and become the catalyst for justice. David Jackson's famous image of Emmett Till's open casket motivated many to join the Civil Rights movement. The images of George Floyd's murder sparked the Black Lives Matter movement of 2020.

Photography has the power to move the needle of justice by capturing raw emotion, anger, sadness, and joy in a single moment in time. A single photo can change the course of history. As photographers, we get to be a part of that. But before you can change the world, you have to know how to break into the industry—and it can be tricky without the knowledge I'm going to share with you.

If you picked up this book, I'm betting you love photography enough to pursue a career in it, but you have no idea where to start. That's where I come in. I want to be the resource and mentor I never had, so you don't have to learn the hard way. I'll be sharing the insider secrets of the photography industry that they don't teach you in school. Because combining your passion for photography with a career can get a little messy. Being a great photographer is only *half* the battle. To thrive in this industry, you need to be a savvy entrepreneur, too. And that's why I took it upon myself to fill in this much-needed gap. Instead of hoping things will change, it's time we take control of our careers—and I'm here to help you do just that. This book will equip you with everything you need to know for a successful photography career. But you have to show up and put in the work.

The photo hustle is *real*. These days, it's not enough to have talent. You have to know the industry—and it's a tough one to break into. Most photography schools and workshops don't teach you how to run a successful business. Rather, they focus on the latest gear and techniques. They'll teach you about posing, directing clients, composition, and lighting. They'll show you all the pretty editing tricks and how to set up a shot.

But *actual* business skills? That stuff *rarely* gets taught in the photography world. Marketing and branding? *Not in most curricula.* Sales and pricing strategies? *I don't think so.* Client experience and retention? *Doubtful.* Financial planning and management? *I'm not seeing it.* Most photographers are expected to figure it out on their own, often through trial and error. But in reality, most photographers were never prepared for the "photo hustle" that exists on the flip side of their passion... I know I wasn't.

If this sounds all too familiar to you, this may be what your journey has looked like up to this point:

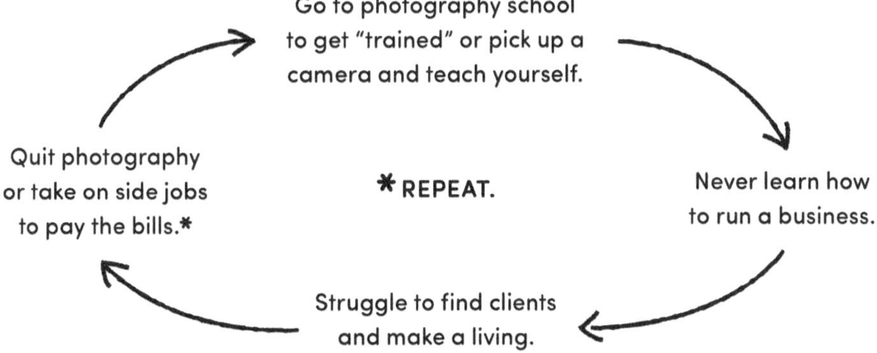

Listen, I know you have the passion. I know you've dedicated your time to your craft. And I know you're ready to get out there and share it with the world. Yes, photography is a tough road. But if you stick it out, get up when you get knocked down, and keep going, you *can* succeed. Keep pushing, keep creating, and keep capturing life through your lens. The world is waiting to see *your* visual eye.

...

Before we jump into the juice, I want to make a quick disclaimer: you may have heard the terms "commercial photography" and "brand photography" used interchangeably. Commercial photography was heavily used in the '90s and early 2000s to describe the art of shooting advertisements for brands in tech, entertainment, fashion, and more. Today, the industry uses "brand photography" instead. I will be using this new term throughout the book.

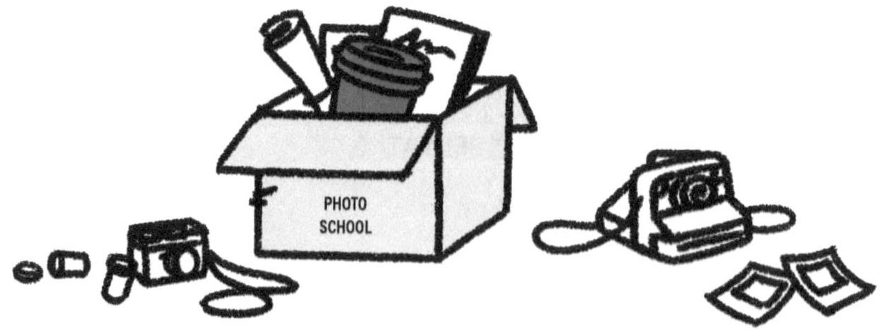

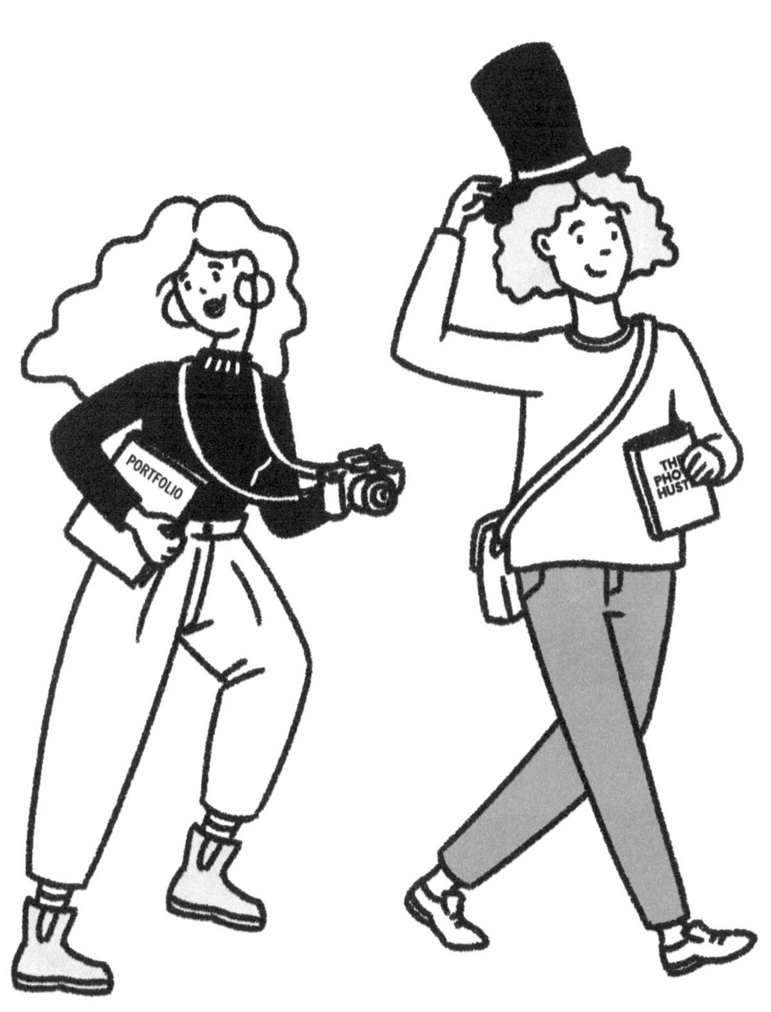

INTRODUCTION

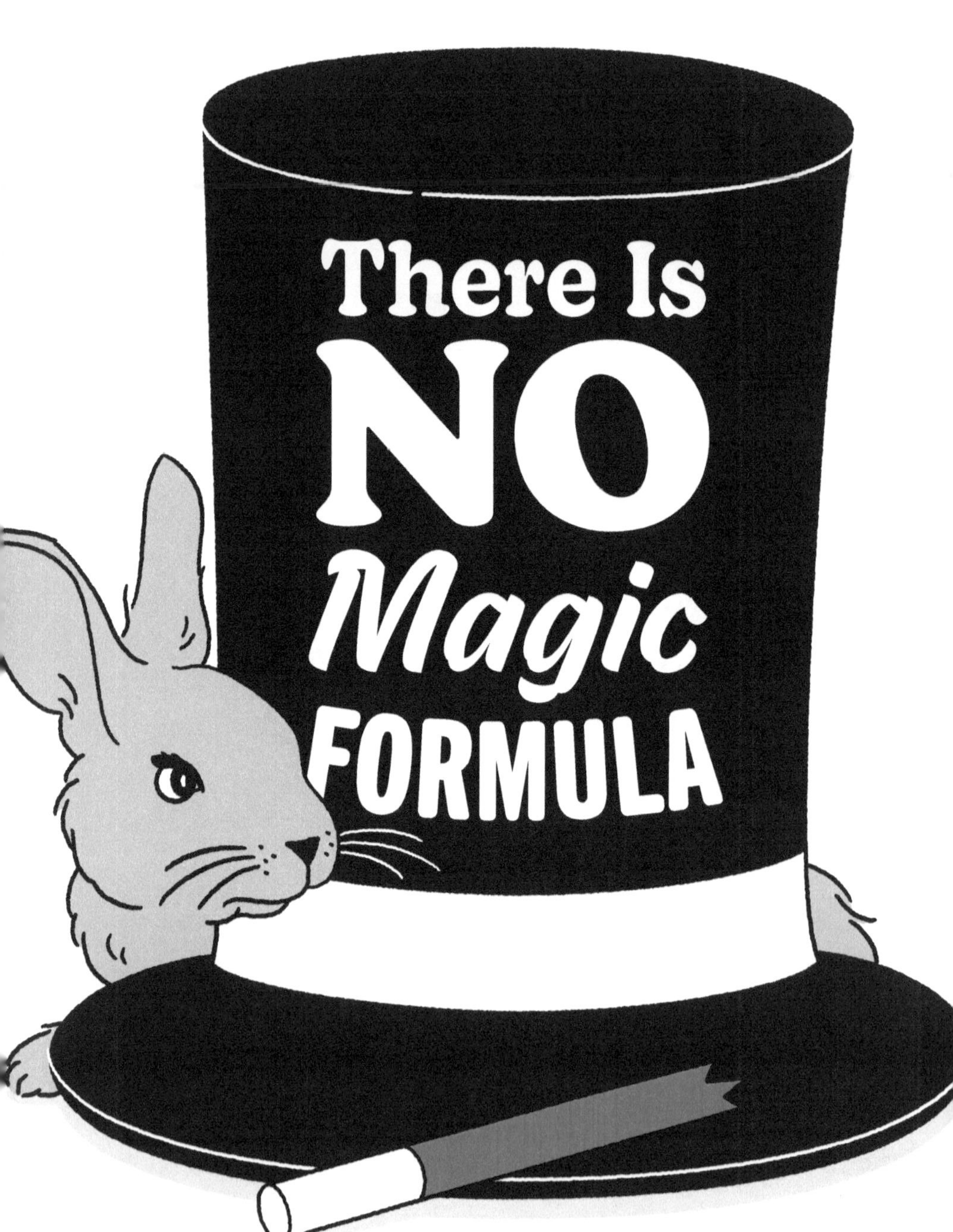

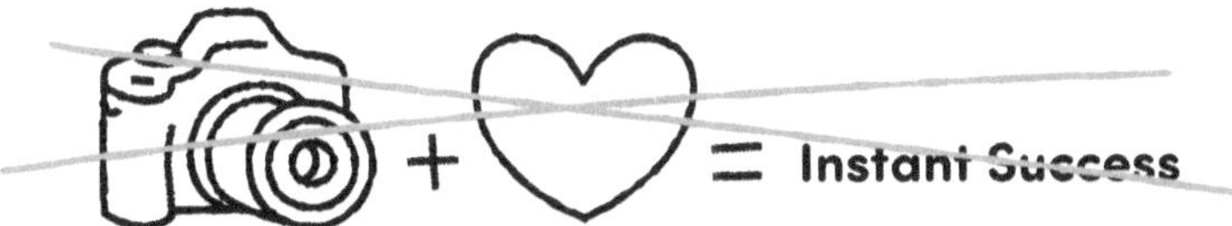

There is no magic formula for making it in photography. If you're hoping for a perfect path to success from Point A to Point B, I'm sorry to be the one to break it to you—it just doesn't exist. No two photographers fall into success in the same way.

"I've done everything right, but nothing is working. *How do I get in?*"

It's a question I get almost daily, but this time it came from a friend—let's call her Michelle—over coffee. Michelle, an incredibly gifted photographer, had been struggling. Two years out of photography school, and she hadn't landed her dream gigs...or anything close to them. Instead, she was building a business photographing families and pets. She was good—damn good—but it wasn't her dream. Like so many photographers I talk to every day, Michelle had talent and drive, but couldn't break into the industry. So, what gives?

I told Michelle what I tell all photographers: the industry has secrets they don't want you to know. No matter how good you are or how many boxes you check, breaking in is tough. And if you don't know what I'm going to share with you on these pages, then your chances of getting in are just as slim. Some photographers make it by luck, some hustle, and some are "discovered." But believe me, there's no perfect path, no magic formula—just straight talent and lots (and lots) of hustle.

• • •

When I was studying for my BFA, my dream was to shoot the cover of *Rolling Stone* magazine. That dream was shaken when, in September 2023, the president and founder Jan Wenner dismissed Black and female artists as not "articulate enough" for his book *The Masters*, a collection of interviews with rock's greatest.[2] His words hit hard, sparking the same frustration I felt following the George Floyd tragedy and the hollow promises made in light of his death. After fifteen years in the industry, I had become accustomed to being one of the few Black people on set, and I began to question why so many talented, hard-working photographers of all kinds were being sidelined. The answer is simple: the industry keeps a lot of information locked away. And I had become a part of the industry-wide gatekeeping that I hated so much. This book is the product of my determination to change that.

Spoiler alert: I'm not a professional photographer—I'm the person behind the scenes, hiring photographers, shaping art direction, and building brand stories big and small. I'm living my dream as a photo editor. Over the last fifteen years, I've had the opportunity to work for *WIRED*, *Southern Living*, Netflix, *AARP*, *MasterClass*, *Square*, and *San Francisco Magazine*. But the journey wasn't easy—I faced a ton of job rejections that nearly shattered my confidence. But I refused to let them break me down—I chose not to let others dictate my worth or my future in the field. So, I took matters into my own hands and hustled hard for *years*. I even changed jobs fourteen times in sixteen years, transforming each of my setbacks into an opportunity to learn, grow, and improve my craft. My journey of hustle and hard work led me to where I am today. I even founded my company, Black Visual Queen, to change the industry and help photographers like you find their path to success in this highly gate-kept arena, where opportunities are often so elusive.

First, a word of warning: this is a tough industry, and brand photography isn't for everyone. The road to that dream is a long one, paved with hustle, hard work, and lots (and lots) of rejection. But since you're reading this book, I'm willing to bet that knowing this doesn't deter you. You're one of the photographers who have the determination to work with prestigious, big-name clients, and you're not ready to throw in the towel on your dream just yet. If this is you, then listen up, because I'm going to teach you everything you need to know about the photo hustle—and how to get in. The photo industry is not just reserved for the elite; it's for anyone willing to do the work. All you need is a little tenacity, talent (which you have), and the tips and tricks I'm going to spill in this book.

DON'T THROW IN THE TOWEL

Through the years, I've seen top photographers ready to quit, exhausted by fierce competition and overwhelmed by technology. Many don't know how to market themselves. So, if you're frustrated by rejections, ghosting, or "we'll keep your name on file" responses, just keep going. Keep hustling, keep honing your craft. The challenges are real, but don't let them extinguish your passion. Embrace your uniqueness, stay motivated, and don't fall into the comparison trap. Photography is rewarding, and the world is waiting to see *your* unique perspective.

"I'll admit it's harder than ever to make it in photography. There's less and less work to go around and less money to be made. So, you really have to be sure you *love* doing this and just know it will be hard sometimes. *Lots* of hills and valleys. If you have enough talent and perseverance, that usually finds a way. Don't give up! At the end of the day, you will have made magic."

—GREG GARRY, PHOTO CREATIVE DIRECTOR AND PRODUCER

SO, WHAT CAN YOU EXPECT FROM THIS BOOK?

In the following pages, you'll learn everything photography school didn't teach you and all the industry secrets the insiders don't share. This is *the* book I wish I'd had back when I was starting out in photography: the tell-all (well, maybe not all—I've signed a lot of non-disclosure agreements!) about the photography biz, especially for editorial and brand work.

The book is split into two parts. Part 1 covers how to get in the room—in other words, how to break into the industry, how to pitch, how to market yourself, handle finances, and land the gig. We'll be diving into your "why" as a photographer because knowing that helps you make the next right decision.

Part 2 explains what to do once you're hired—how to navigate estimates, contracts, agents, photoshoot etiquette, avoid the dreaded blacklist (yes, it's real), and how to redeem yourself if you find yourself on it.

Consider this book your trusted mentor. I want this to be the book you reach for when you land the gig and have no idea what an estimate looks like or what to watch out for in a contract. I want you to take this everywhere with you. Carry it in your purse. Stow it in your camera bag. Use it as a resource to help you navigate the tough business side of photography. By the end, I want you to feel encouraged, equipped, and confident to build the successful photography career you've always dreamed of.

Ready to find your "magic formula?" Let's dive in.

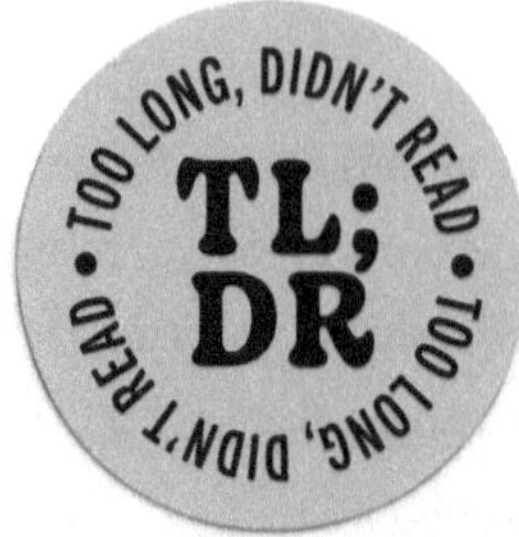

At the end of every chapter, you'll find a TLDR section for easy reference to the key points.

This section will be your best friend and your go-to for quick takeaways, including:

- I'm not going to sugarcoat it: this industry is *tough*, and brand photography isn't for everyone.

- The rejections will come, but you *have* to hustle!

- The frustration you're feeling is real. But don't throw in the towel just yet. Keep working on your craft and keep pushing forward.

- Don't let the challenges dim your passion for photography!

- Embrace your individuality, stay motivated, and don't you dare compare yourself to others!

- There is no magic formula for the perfect photography career.

- There are industry secrets they don't want you to know, and I'm going to share them all.

- This book will empower you to continue pursuing the craft you fell in love with — and do it successfully.

PART 1
HOW TO GET IN THE ROOM

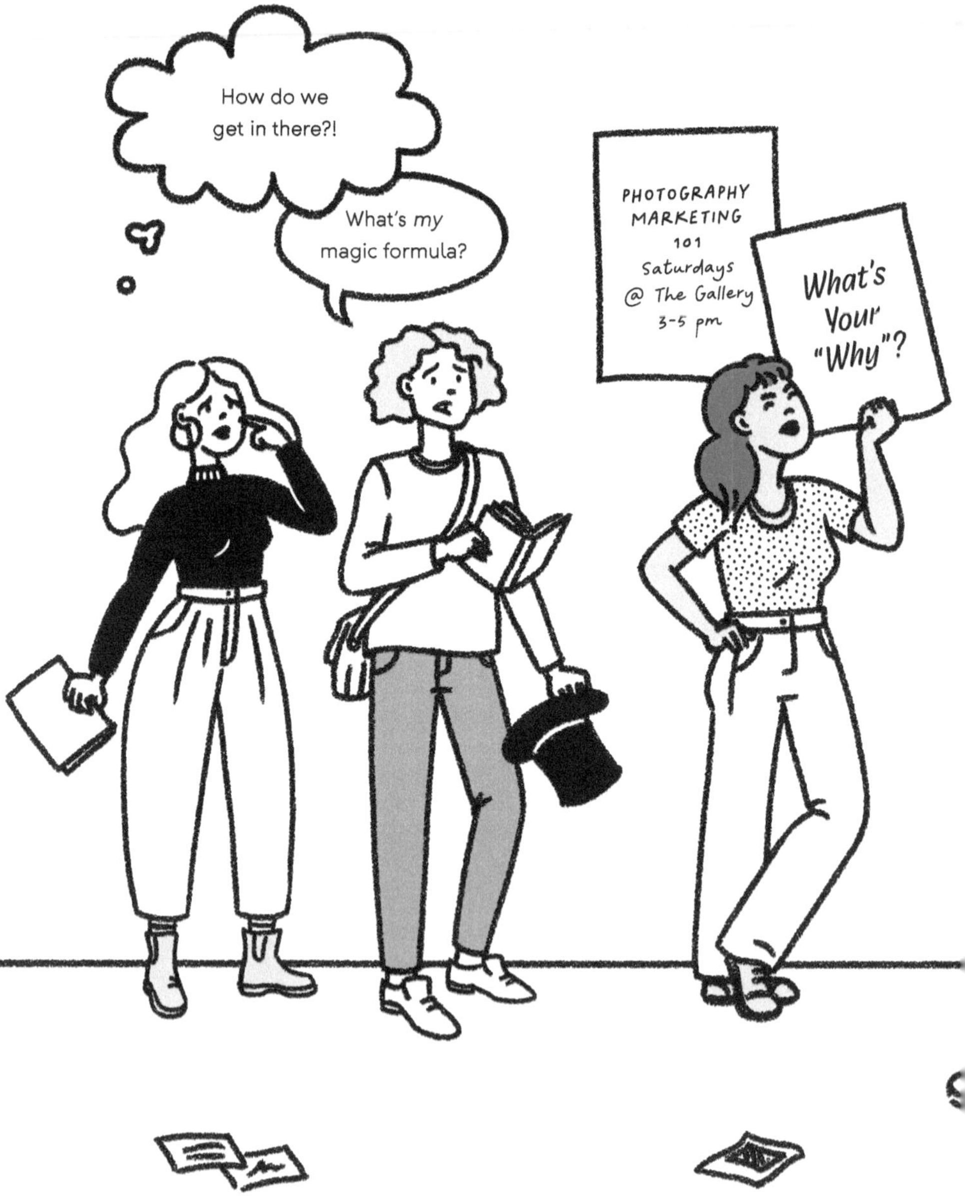

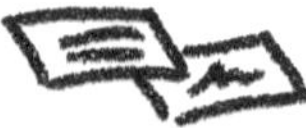

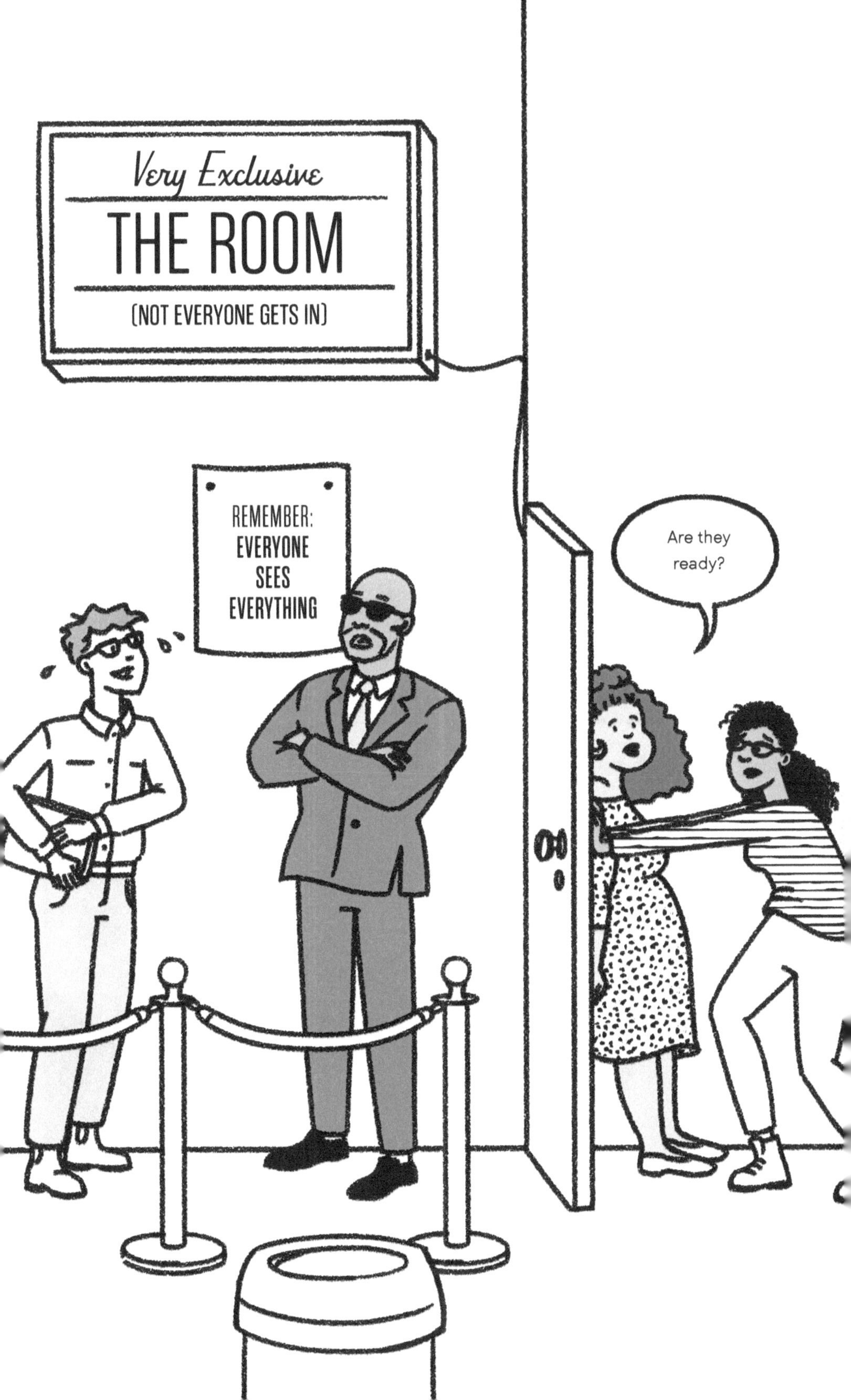

Very Exclusive
THE ROOM
(NOT EVERYONE GETS IN)
REMEMBER:
EVERYONE
SEES
EVERYTHING
Are they ready?

CHAPTER 1

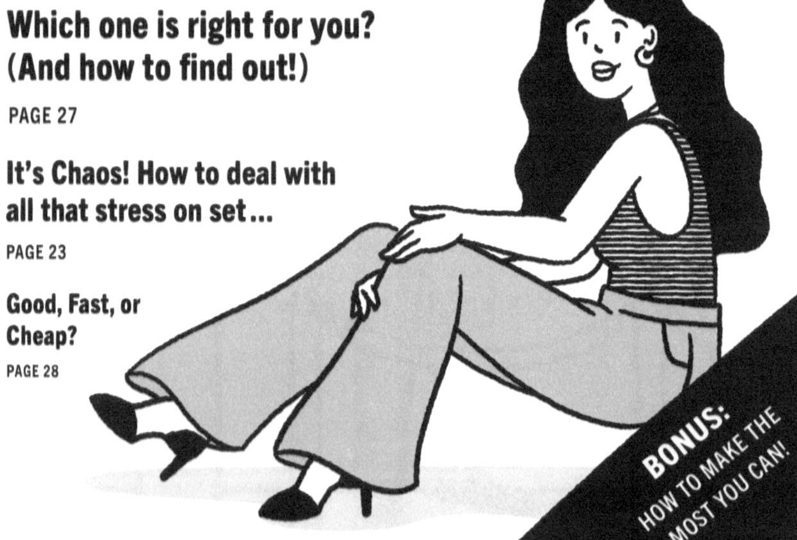

FALL • $7.99
Budgets!?
Help!
PAGE 29
SO, YOU WANT TO SHOOT FOR
BRANDS
and Editorial?
Which one is right for you?
(And how to find out!)
PAGE 27
It's Chaos! How to deal with
all that stress on set…
PAGE 23
Good, Fast, or
Cheap?
PAGE 28
BONUS:
HOW TO MAKE THE
MOST YOU CAN!

"If you're in it for the money,
then you've already lost."

—BLACK VISUAL QUEEN

Most photographers come to me wanting to know how to make lots of money, but as it turns out, photography isn't what it used to be. Both brand and editorial companies are looking for quality work for the least amount of money, and as the one doing the hiring, I see this challenge firsthand. Before we dive into brand versus editorial photography, there's one truth you need to know: if you're in it for the money, you've already lost.

When you build a career, passion is what keeps you going. You need a strong reason to pursue photography—one that goes beyond financial reward. Know your "why" and what you're worth, and build your career on those two things. Your why will keep you motivated on long, tough days and guide your choices in this challenging industry. To make it far in this career, you've *got* to know your why.

KNOW YOUR WHY

If you want to be a successful photographer (and I know you do), you need to know exactly what you love about photography and the why behind your passion. Why do you love photography? What about it makes your heart come alive? What keeps you reaching for your camera day after day? Knowing your why will keep you resilient through challenging times. (And believe me, there will be many.)

It's also an important compass, guiding you on which jobs to accept and which ones aren't worth your time. Knowing your why will help you recognize the value you bring, allowing you to set boundaries and choose the right opportunities.

$$(\text{👓} + (+/- \text{💵})) \times \heartsuit = \text{Why?}$$

KNOW YOUR WORTH

Over the last fifteen years of my career, I've learned that "know your worth" has become a powerful mantra that resonates with most of us—especially women. It encourages us to recognize and embrace the immense value we bring to the world. Let's face it: this industry can be tough. It often undervalues your skills and the impact you have on others. This is why truly knowing your worth goes beyond money or recognition.

Instead, it's about setting boundaries and being selective with the opportunities you decide to pursue, ensuring they align with what you deserve both financially and creatively. Embracing your worth means committing to growth, honing your skills, and staying ahead of the game. You bring so much value to this industry! But when you're starting out, it's easy to get taken advantage of. By embracing your value and worth, you'll be able to call it as you see it and make confident decisions that propel you toward your dreams, not away from them.

BRANDS VS. EDITORIAL: WHAT'S THE DIFFERENCE?

The first step to breaking into the photography industry is knowing what part of the industry you want to pursue: brand or editorial photography. To the untrained eye, the terms may seem similar or interchangeable; however, each area has different objectives. Knowing which path suits you best will shape how you present yourself and your work. So...which one is right for you?

BRAND PHOTOGRAPHY

Imagine with me for a moment: you're on location for a week-long shoot where everyone is relaxing on a private island or a poolside in LA, shooting bikini-clad talent for the latest fragrance fresh out of Paris and ending the day precisely at 4:00 p.m. with a strawberry daiquiri in hand. You do these gigs two or three times a year, and you're financially set, but you still book more shoots because your work is basically a vacation.

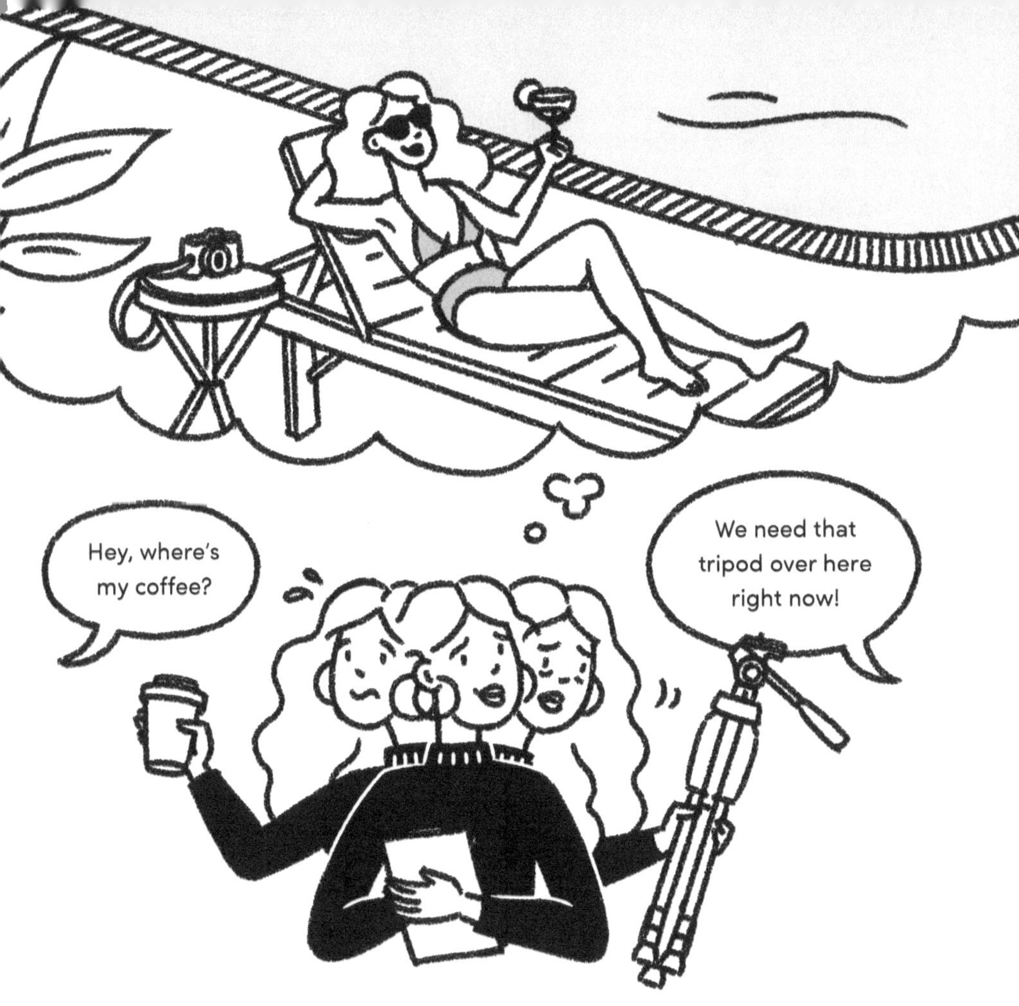

Put down this book immediately and go splash some cold water on your face because you're waking up to the new reality. What I've just described was the industry twenty years ago, but today, budget cuts have also cut the fantasy. Sure, you can still make good money working as a brand photographer, but the job is no longer relaxed week-long shoots. No. Today, these are jam-packed, wall-to-wall, twelve-hour days of getting it done because *time is money*. You're given a very specific deliverable for your client, and you either hit that deliverable or you're out. Do not pass Go, do *not* collect $200.

Brand photography focuses on promoting or selling a product, service, or brand. It's widely used in advertising campaigns, marketing materials, product catalogs, websites, and other promotional platforms. Brand photographers work closely with clients to create images that reflect and enhance their brand identity. Shoots are often carefully staged and curated, with an emphasis on product presentation, visual appeal, and persuasive impact.

As a brand photographer, you'll typically work with larger budgets, given the close link between marketing and advertising investments. Success in this field can lead to long-term collaborations and recurring assignments with clients or agencies—a dream for many, right?

However, the trade-off for big budgets and long-term engagements is client demands and constraints, which may limit your artistic freedom and personal expression. It's also a *highly* competitive field, requiring constant self-promotion, strong client relationships, and a solid grasp of industry trends at all times. To say there's a lot of pressure to produce is an understatement. Your images must align precisely with the client's brand or marketing goals—and there's no room for error.

EDITORIAL PHOTOGRAPHY

In contrast, editorial photography focuses on creating images that tell a story or support a narrative in magazines, newspapers, and other editorial platforms. It often accompanies an article, offering visual depth and additional context to a story highlighting current events, social issues, lifestyle, fashion, or culture. This style may involve photojournalism, documentary-style photography, or editorial portraiture tailored to the subject matter and the publication's chosen aesthetic. Many photographers are drawn to editorial work because of the creative freedom it offers. But here's the caveat: you won't get paid the big bucks associated with commercial brand projects.

As an editorial photographer, you'll have the power to evoke emotions, raise awareness, and educate audiences on social, cultural, or political issues through the images you produce. The reward for this work often comes in exposure and recognition, as your images can be published in reputable magazines or newspapers, opening doors to future opportunities. However, editorial photography typically involves tighter budgets since it isn't directly tied to marketing campaigns, making it challenging for photographers to rely solely on these assignments for income.

If editorial photography is your passion, keep in mind that the availability of paid editorial assignments can be competitive, especially for emerging photographers. Not only that, but editorial publications often have the final say on image selection and placement, which can limit your control over how your work appears. But more on that later on.

WHICH ONE IS RIGHT FOR ME?

The decision on whether to pursue brand or editorial photography is solely up to you! Most photographers end up doing a mix of both, often focusing on brand for financial reasons. As a photographer, you don't have to choose one over the other. However, each requires a different approach to marketing yourself, so it's essential to consider both paths as you develop your portfolio. And as with most things, one of the biggest deciding factors for many photographers is simple: it comes down to the money.

IT'S ALL ABOUT THE BUDGET

Every incredible image you see in a magazine or brand campaign starts with one key element: the budget. The dollar amount guides the photographer and photo editor, defining the team size, locations, and timeline for the project. In short, a budget outlines how the work will get done.

Think of budgets as the blueprint for the deliverables. The first step in making beautiful art is figuring out the money. For creatives, this is part of the journey: to make money from art. It's important to note, however, that on set, everything is subject to change. A stakeholder might ask for an unplanned shot, and you'll need to consult the budget to make that happen.

In brand photography, there's an iron triangle. Its three sides are good, fast, and cheap. There is a caveat, though—you can only ever have two. It's your job as the photographer to understand which two your client has chosen and to communicate the trade-offs clearly. If they want their photoshoot to be good and fast, it won't be cheap. If they want it to be cheap and fast, the quality will suffer. And if they want the shoot to be good and cheap, they're not paying for it to be fast. Clarifying this with clients upfront is essential.

In my role, I often have to tell stakeholders, "Hey, we can do this, but it will cost more." If they're set on keeping it under budget, I'll ask if they're okay with a possible dip in quality. Some stakeholders want a fast shoot with a quick turnaround, which raises day rates for the photographer and crew, making it more expensive. The budget tells us the answer to these questions. When you look at that, the answer will be simple.

Production people understand, live, and die by this principle...until they get on set. Then, everyone wants everything! It always amazes me how often clients expect to add countless tasks without adjusting the budget, timeline, or quality of what they are proposing. Clarifying and restating which two sides of the iron triangle the client has prioritized is key to staying on budget and maintaining your integrity as a photographer.

THE IRON TRIANGLE*

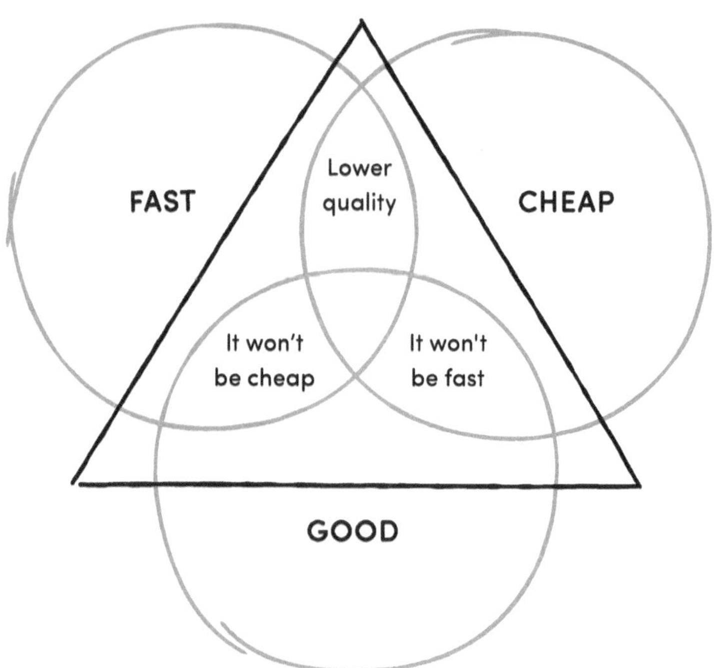

✳ You can only ever have two.

BRAND AND EDITORIAL EXAMPLE BUDGETS

The following are sample budgets for brand photoshoots to help you visualize how to work within different budget ranges as a photographer. Since budget cuts are more common than not these days, consider how you would accomplish each shoot on the lower end of the budget, and then imagine what you would do with the maximum allowed. Oftentimes, clients will expect you to meet all their objectives on a tight budget, so mastering a shoot with minimal lights, props, and crew is essential.

BRAND PHOTOGRAPHY:

Product Campaign: Showcasing a specific product, either for print or digital advertising purposes.
Budget range: $10,000–$100,000+ depending on the scale and complexity.

Corporate Business: Creating images for corporate websites, brochures, or marketing material.
Budget range: $5,000–$20,000.

Food and Beverage: Capturing images of food and drinks for menus, cookbooks, or advertising campaigns.
Budget range: $5,000–$15,000.

Architectural/Interior: Shooting interiors or exteriors of buildings for real estate companies or home decor brands.
Budget range: $5,000–$30,000, depending on the size and location of the project.

GENERAL RATES FOR CREW:

On-Set Photographer:
Entry-level: $500–$2,000 per day
Experienced: $2,000–$10,000 per day
High-end or celebrity photographers: $5,000–$50,000+ per day

Assistant Photographer:
Entry-level: $100–$300 per day
Experienced: $250–$500 per day
Specialized or technical assistants: $400–$800+ per day

Digital Technician:
Entry-level: $200–$500 per day
Experienced: $500–$1,500 per day

Specialized or advanced technicians:
$1,500–$3,500+ per day

Producer:
Entry-level: $500–$1,500 per day
Experienced: $1,500–$5,000 per day
Senior or high-level producers:
$5,000–$20,000+ per day

Retoucher:
Entry-level: $150–$300 per hour
Experienced: $300–$500 per hour
High-end or renowned retouchers:
$500–$1,500+ per hour

EDITORIAL PHOTOSHOOTS:

Fashion Editorial: This could involve shooting the latest fashion trends for a magazine spread.
Budget range: $5,000–$20,000.

Beauty Editorial: Focuses on capturing makeup or skincare products and showcasing beauty trends.
Budget range: $3,000–$15,000.

Lifestyle Editorial: Involves capturing a specific lifestyle or theme, such as travel, food, fitness, or home decor.
Budget range: $4,000–$10,000.

Celebrity Editorial: Featuring a well-known personality for a magazine cover or feature.
Budget range: $10,000–$50,000+ depending on the celebrity.

Portrait Editorial: One-page feature.
Budget range: $500–$800.

News and Current Events: $200–$500 per day.

A NOTE FROM KAREN:

Please note that these budget ranges are approximate and will vary depending on factors such as location, talent fees, production requirements, and any additional services required. These numbers are all based on the industry in the United States and serve as a general guide. They will need to be researched based on your location and specific situation. Budgets are not standardized because each company has its own requirements and resources. Some have huge budgets; others, smaller ones. Sometimes, the money offered makes sense,

and it's all a go! Other times, photographers may feel the budget is too low for the effort required, or they may lack the passion for the project to justify taking it on. If the budget doesn't feel right, remember that it's always okay to pass on a job.

BUDGETS TREND WITH THE ECONOMY

When the economy is good, budgets are ample. People just aren't looking at numbers as closely. They're more flexible and don't mind increasing the budget to accommodate more creativity. However, when we're in a recession, budgets get slashed—*hard*.

I started my career in 2008, just as the economy was cratering, so I quickly learned how the global economy impacts in-house budgets and decision-making. No one prepared me for this in school! The creative department is usually among the first teams to get hit with budget cuts, often leading to smaller teams and heavier workloads.

If you're working with a limited budget, it's likely not because the company doesn't want to pay you well but because their internal resources have been obliterated. Even with long-standing clients, expect day rates to be renegotiated during economic downturns. This trend became especially prominent during COVID-19: budgets were cut, and every expense required more justification.

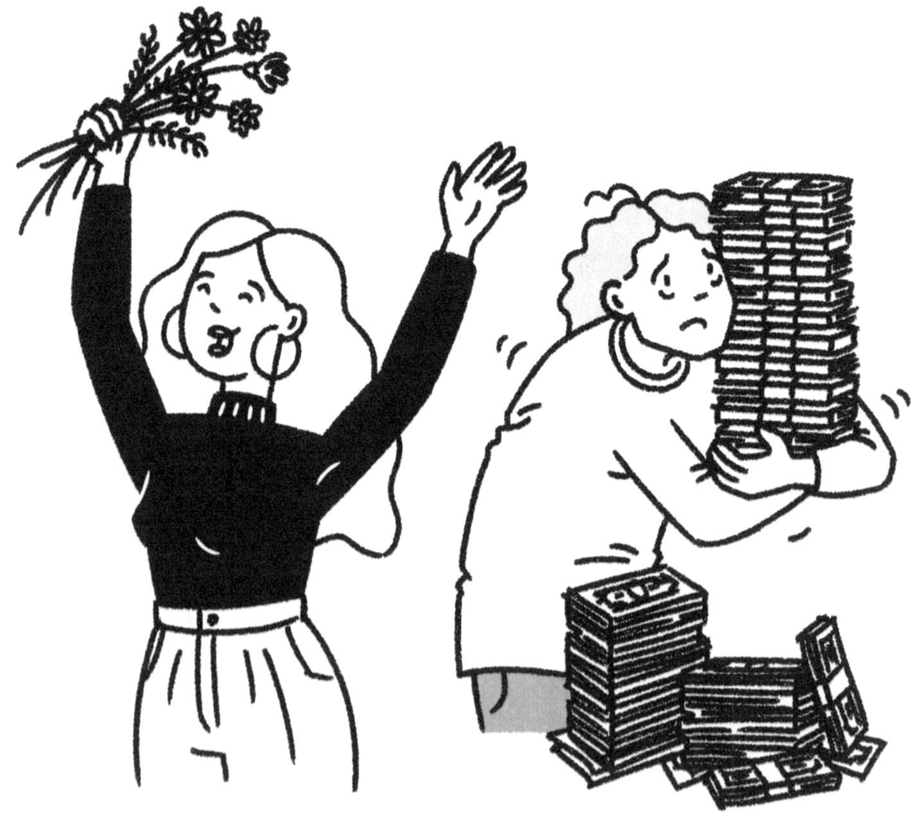

SHOULD I TAKE THE JOB?

It comes down to two things: creativity vs. money. As a photographer, it's up to you to decide whether a budget makes a job worth taking. The Iron Triangle can help here. Personally, I'm always upfront with photographers about the budget—because that's just my nature. If it's low, I'll ask, "What can we adjust to make this budget work?" But many companies won't do that—they'll set a budget and a list of demands and expect you to deliver. This is the moment you decide if you stay for the gig or if you need to walk away: does this job make you feel valued, or does it feel like settling?

Low budgets are a hot topic in the photography world lately. There are companies with a standard crappy day rate, and that tends to drive rates down across the board because there's always someone who's going to take that low rate—just for the experience. It's up to you to decide if the rate is worth it or if this job can lead to higher-paying gigs in the future.

Early on in my career, I moved from the East Coast to the West Coast for a low-paying editorial job. It was a massive pay cut. But I built my portfolio and laid the foundation for my future career. Did I have to work other jobs to make ends meet? Absolutely. But it was all worth it in the end.

Photography is often a freelance or side gig for many people, so when budgets tighten or during downturns, think about your financial stability. Listen: it's okay if you need to take a 9–5 job. You are not a failure. It can help you build a safety net until you're ready to focus on photography again. Talk to a professional attorney, accountant, or financial advisor for advice tailored to your specific situation.

Do what you need to make ends meet, and be willing to pivot season after season. The early days are for building your portfolio and setting up a runway for your future. You'll thank yourself later—trust me.

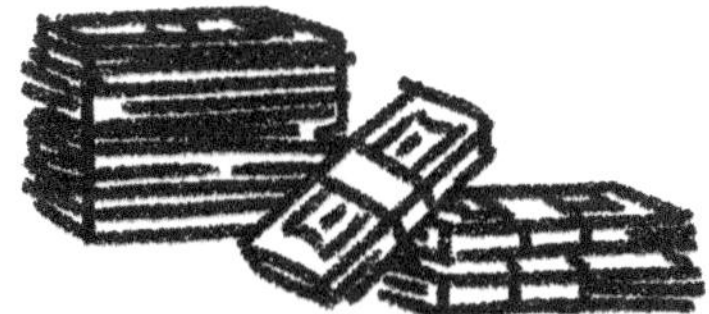

ARE YOU WILLING TO WALK AWAY?

Many photographers in the hustle forget that they have the power to walk away. At the end of the day, it's all about dollars and cents, and these numbers can change quickly with the industry, company, and season. The question you need to be asking yourself is this: does the rate justify your work? If the answer is yes, that's great!

This is why knowing your value is *crucial*. If you're on a solid diet of ramen noodles, you may not have the luxury of turning down gigs. But if you're in a position to turn down low-paying gigs, do so with confidence—there will *always* be more opportunities.

Now that you understand the distinctions between the brand and editorial photography industries, take a moment to reflect on which path suits you best. We'll build on this in the next chapter, so knowing who you are as a photographer is key to moving forward. In Chapter 2, we'll dive into building your brand, finding your niche, and creating a website that captures the attention of your dream clients.

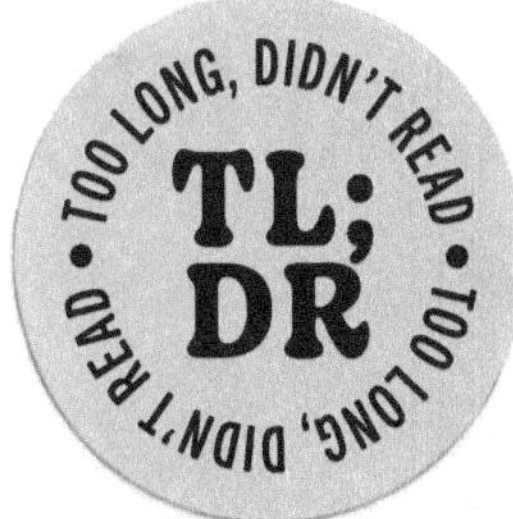

- If you're in it for the money, you've already lost.

- Know your why! This will help you set boundaries and be more selective in the opportunities you decide to pursue.

- Don't settle for less than what you deserve.
  (Financially *and* creatively.)

- Decide if you want to pursue brand or editorial photography.

- Brand photography is primarily focused on promoting or selling a product, service, or brand.

- Editorial photography is about creating images that help tell a story in magazines, newspapers, and other publications.

- There's more money in brand photography, but you don't have to choose one over the other. You can do both!

- Budgets fluctuate with the economy.

- You're not a failure if you have to take a 9–5 job.
  (Those bills don't pay themselves!)

CHAPTER 2

It's All About

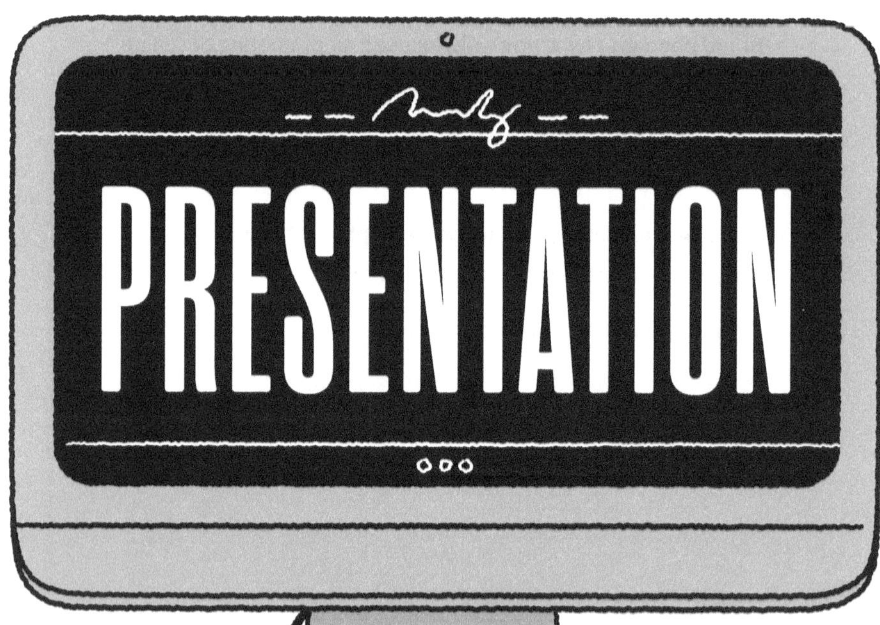

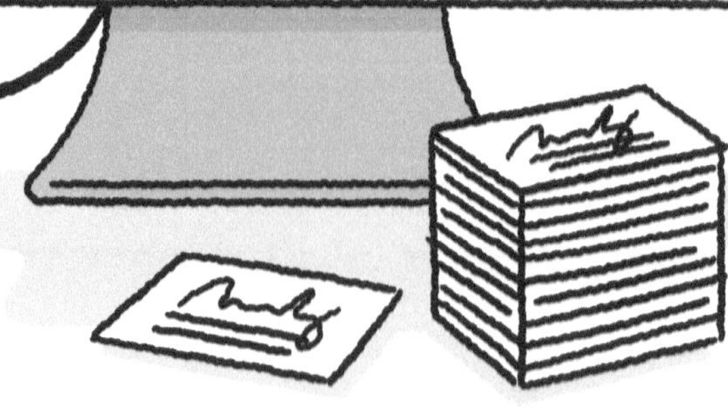

PRESENTATION

"Presentation is everything! Well... almost.
It's like 90 percent. The other 10 percent?
Being able to deliver the quality of work
we see on your website."

—BLACK VISUAL QUEEN

You might have a great eye for light and color, but it means zilch in this industry if you can't get in the room for a shot at a job—and that takes more work upfront than most realize. Presentation is *everything*. It's what lands gigs, keeps them coming, and keeps you off the blacklist. Getting in the room is one thing, but how you show up and deliver determines whether you'll keep landing your dream gigs.

Years ago, I was in one of my first jobs, working as a photo editor for an incredible magazine, and was tasked with finding a photographer to shoot a local celebrity in the food industry. I was excited to give some new talent a chance to shine. I found a photographer with some celebrity portraits of Jay-Z on his website. Granted, they were a bit dated, but promising. I sent his site to my team, and everyone gave me the green light, so I booked him.

On the day of the shoot, I was completely caught off guard. I watched as this photographer pulled out an ancient camera. What he didn't pull out of his bag was a lightbox or softbox. No flash. Nothing. I thought, *At least he has a camera. Maybe he can make this work.* I approached him to check in, only for him to tell me he wouldn't speak to me directly—only to his so-called "assistant," a friend he had brought along.

My yellow flags turned bright red at this point, and when I saw the final images, my worst fears were confirmed: they were unusable. Our budget was spent, and we had no viable photos. Needless to say, this photographer's website presence did *not* match his on-site presence. *I was bamboozled.*

Listen: once you break that trust, it's hard to regain it. If you don't show up as your best professional self, as your website promises, it's unlikely that you'll get another recommendation from me in the future.

BUILDING YOUR BRAND

Like it or not, you are a brand. As a photographer, how you present yourself to the world is how the world will perceive you. The question is: are you authentically representing yourself through your website, portfolio, and social media channels? To succeed, you must show up as your best self—both online and in person. And it all starts with building a brand that is authentic to who you are.

FIND YOUR NICHE

One key to building your brand is identifying your niche, or as I like to call it, your "secret sauce." Many photographers don't know what their niche is—and that's okay! But it's something you want to discover. Remember: you can't be everything to everyone. That gets you nowhere. You'll end up feeling spread thin and uninspired.

Finding your niche not only strengthens your brand but also creates a unique experience for clients and future clients. When you specialize, clients remember you as the "go-to" in that area. It becomes a memorable experience, and clients will proudly say they worked with you.

Don't know what your secret sauce is yet? That's okay! This is your time to explore, experiment, and try new things until you figure it out. Remember, you can't build an authentic brand unless you explore the world, shoot in new ways, and do your market research. This is your opportunity to discover what you truly enjoy, what doesn't resonate with you, and why.

If you want to be a portrait photographer, study the greats throughout history. Look at what made them exceptional—their unique spin, style, and techniques. The same strategy applies to any type of photography. Study the masters in that niche, examine your competition, and learn from other photographers who inspire you.

Then, use this knowledge to develop your own style. Once you find your niche, people will seek you out for your distinctive style.

Before we move on, I do want to say this: no one wants a copycat. When I hire for a brand gig, I'm looking for photographers with genuine talent and a unique style and spin. So, when you're doing your market research, don't use it as an opportunity to copy what others are doing. No client will say, "I like what you do. Can you do it like so-and-so?" They don't want the cheaper version of someone else. Bring your unique vision to every project, and deliver what only *you* can do.

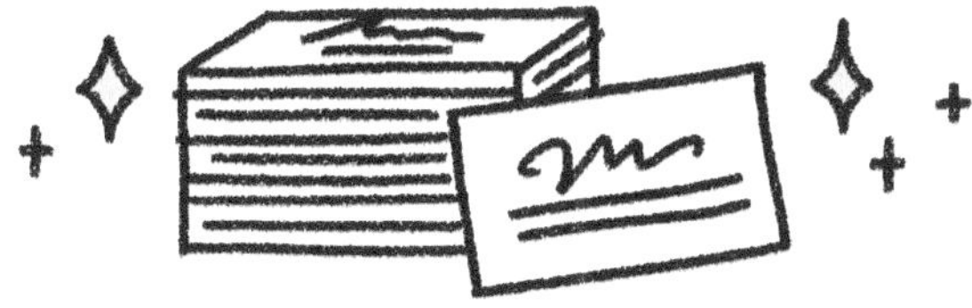

YOUR WEBSITE
IS YOUR BUSINESS CARD

Your website is your main marketing vehicle. It's your business card, portfolio, and the critical first impression to securing your next gig. In ninety seconds, it must showcase your work, individual style, and why clients should hire you.

People can usually tell the difference between a good photo and a bad one, even if they can't explain why—it's *that* spark you want them to feel when they visit your site. You want them to see something special. Something unique. Something that draws them in. If you're not landing the clients or jobs you want, most of the time, your website will be the reason.

As a photo editor, I review *hundreds* of websites weekly. Some are incredible and have me reaching out to the photographer within seconds. Others are awful and leave me feeling like I've wasted my time. In this industry, time is money, so if you want to catch the eye of photo editors, creative directors, agents, and potential clients, read on.

INSIDER TIPS:

"Be clear and specific about what only you can offer — with subject matter, aesthetic, personality, etc. Know what makes you unique and bring that to the forefront."

— ASH BARHAMAND, VISUAL MEDIA DIRECTOR AT *THE HOLLYWOOD REPORTER*

"I love a good, clean site that gets to the point. I want to be able to see the photographer's voice very quickly, but I also appreciate it when I can see the potential in someone who might be a little greener. Beyond that, once I know something about the photographer, then it's in how they carry themselves as a human. If I already know that they have the technical skills and the eye, then the thing that will make me want to hire them (or keep hiring them) is their interpersonal skills. Are they kind? Do they work well with everyone on set? Does the talent feel comfortable around them?"

— KELLY ELAINE GARTHWAITE, FOUNDER OF HEY Y'ALL!

 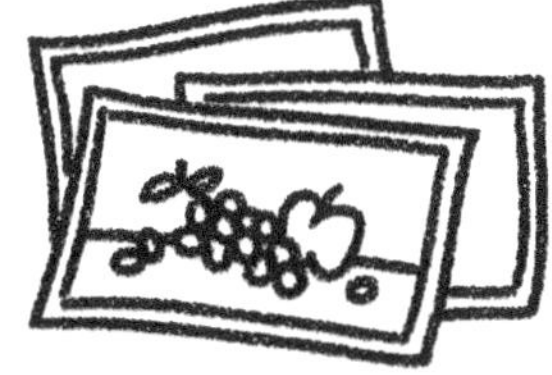

CURATE YOUR WORK TO YOUR DREAM CLIENTS

You need to have a kick-ass portfolio curated to the audience you want to reach. Remember, you can't be everything to everyone. This is where you have to get critical of yourself with an internal audit. Is each piece of work helping you get the jobs you want? If not, take it off. Consider how brand executives—who may not be visually inclined—might interpret your work. Does it speak their language?

Speak the language of your dream clients. Imagine what they'd be looking for, and study their visual style. For instance, if you want to shoot for Nike, skip the food photography. If high-end brands like Tiffany & Co. or Prada are your targets, why do you have your Walmart ads front and center?

I get it: self-editing can be tough. I coach photographers all the time who struggle with the concept of "killing their little darlings." But taking it off your website doesn't mean it's gone forever. Create a separate website for your favorite projects. This will keep them accessible without cluttering your main portfolio. If self-auditing is too hard, ask a trusted mentor or someone in the business for constructive feedback.

INSIDER TIPS:

"Work with an editor or a trusted colleague to help you organize your website and the work you put on it. Include any personal work that speaks to the types of jobs you'd like to get hired for (editorial or brand). If you photograph weddings or families separately from editorial/brand work, then please make a separate website for that work since the intended audiences are entirely separate."

— LAUREN JOSEPH, FREELANCE PHOTO EDITOR

"Make your point of view clear. Being able to shoot beautiful photos is table stakes. Organize and curate your work in a way that helps someone searching for a photographer quickly find relevant parallels in your body of work. Highlight your strongest work, and don't be afraid to edit out old work or work that doesn't represent where you want to go."

— CHRISTINA COOKSEY, FOUNDER OF CEILING TRAIN

"I sincerely believe in portfolio reviews. I know that they can be very expensive, but I have always commissioned someone from a review, mainly because you get to know their personality in the worst speed dating way possible. Nerves… It's all out there. But, also, everyone shows work via video conference now. You shouldn't have to fly to NY to show your 'book.' It's okay to contact a photo editor and ask for a Zoom slice in their schedule. It's such a lovely break for us to look at photography and hear from you — it reminds us why we got into this business in the first place. *You.*"

— ANNA GOLDWATER ALEXANDER, DIRECTOR OF PHOTOGRAPHY AT *WIRED*

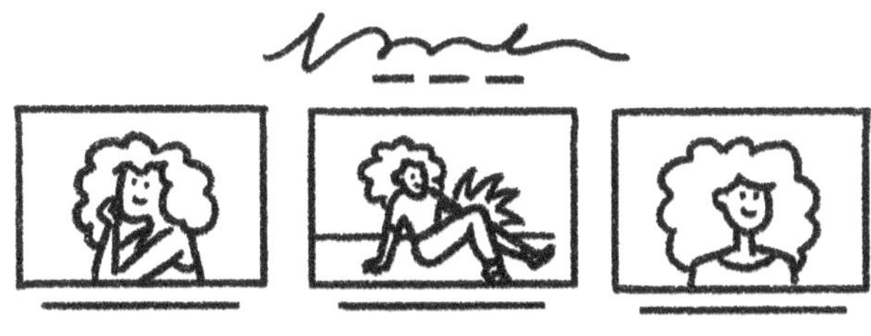

KEEP IT SIMPLE

Your website doesn't have to be over the top—the simpler, the better! One of my biggest pet peeves is websites that are hard to navigate. They end up preventing people from seeing your work (which is what they came to your site for in the first place). My biggest piece of advice? Don't overcomplicate it. Don't try to be fancy, and don't overthink it.

Create a simple, intuitive navigation or menu bar with clear categories, making it easy for visitors to find what they're looking for without too many clicks. Remember, people are there to see your work. An overly complex website that's hard work to navigate shouldn't be the reason you miss out on jobs.

My friend Greg Garry, photo creative director and producer, shared, "Don't over-design. Let the power of the photo speak for itself. Be clear about what your categories are. Be original—never try to emulate someone else's website." He's right. Elaborate designs can be distracting. Greg continued:

> There was a bad trend of overly fussy sites like you were reading a storybook and had to literally turn the pages. That kind of thing drives me insane. You are a photographer, not a web designer. All you need to do is to show the work. No bells and whistles, no music, just photos.

A clean, uncluttered design highlights your work, ensures faster loading times, and encourages visitors to explore more galleries or even book a session with you. And that's exactly what your website is for. So, when it comes to creating your website, keep these three things in mind:

- White space is your friend! Use it to frame your photos beautifully.
- Choose a simple color scheme that complements your unique style.
- Keep navigation straightforward and easy to understand.

At the end of the day, we just want to look at pretty pictures. Don't make it complicated!

INSIDER TIP:

"Start with an overview on the landing page and provide a handful of different edits for your different specializations. Have clear and simple labeling. Poetry and abstract descriptions can be fun elsewhere but not for navigating."

— ASH BARHAMAND, VISUAL MEDIA DIRECTOR AT *THE HOLLYWOOD REPORTER*

LOAD TIMES MATTER!

Picture this: I'm in a meeting, presenting my top picks for our next brand shoot. Four out of five photographers' portfolios load smoothly, but the fifth—the one I was most excited about—just won't load. After waiting and trying again, I had to skip them. That photographer lost out on an opportunity they never even knew they had, all because of slow load times. Don't make that mistake! Whether building a new site or refreshing an existing one, you want to keep load times top of mind. Make sure your site scrolls smoothly, too!

Also, check image quality. Blurry or low-resolution images can cast doubt on your expertise. If it's not something you'd proudly frame, it shouldn't be on your website.

INSIDER TIP:

"I prefer not to have to click 'more.' I love it when it automatically loads the next row."

— REBECCA KARAMEHMEDOVIC, FOUNDER/PARTNER AT SWAY NY

DON'T FORGET ABOUT MOBILE!

These days, almost everyone uses their smartphone to browse the web. Whether it's a potential client searching for a photographer or an art director looking for creative talent, we're likely doing it on our phones. By optimizing your site for mobile devices, you're creating a better user experience—which keeps people on your site for longer. Plus, search engines like Google prioritize mobile-friendly sites, meaning a mobile-optimized portfolio boosts your visibility and increases your chances of getting those coveted gigs. A mobile-friendly website tells potential clients that you're current and focused on making your work look awesome, no matter what device they're using.

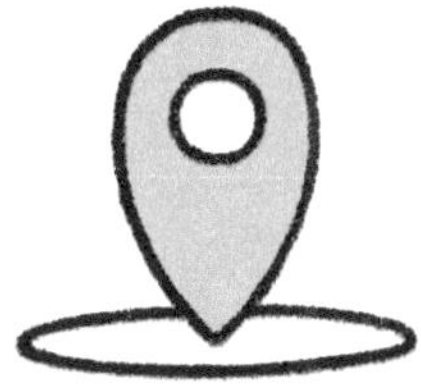

LOCATION, LOCATION, LOCATION

We need to know where you're located! Surprisingly, many photographers forget this important detail. I'll visit a site and see a long backstory about where they were born, how many times they've moved, and the cool locations they've shot. Listen, we don't care! All we need to know is where you're working from *right now!* Stop burying the lead.

Oftentimes, location impacts whether we have the budget to hire you. With tight budgets, we prefer hiring locally to save on travel costs. If you're in LA and our shoot is in New York, knowing your location upfront helps us avoid wasting time if we can't cover travel.

INSIDER TIPS:

"*Location!* Please make your current or primary location *abundantly* clear on your website, on your Instagram, everywhere."

— LAUREN JOSEPH, FREELANCE PHOTO EDITOR

"Make your email address really easy to find, or have a direct link that opens your email in a new window."

— KELLY ELAINE GARTHWAITE, FOUNDER OF HEY Y'ALL!

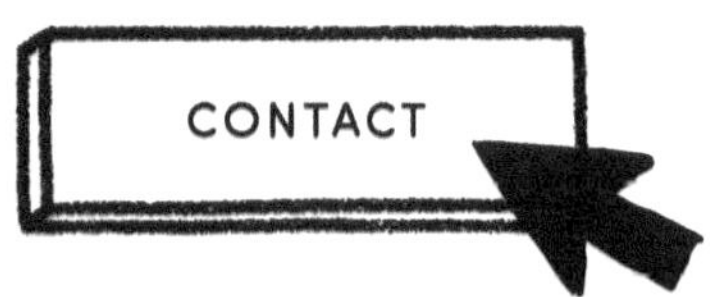

MAKE IT EASY TO CONTACT YOU

You'd be surprised to learn the number of photographers who get passed up for jobs because it's not easy to contact them. List your email directly on your site—it's quicker and more personal than just a form. Forms are very popular but can add layers of security or verification, and it's often unclear if the message even gets through. Make it easy to contact you! If you want to add your phone number, that's great too. But if you're a female, that may get a little sketchy. Use your discretion there. The goal is simple: to ensure potential clients can easily reach out to you.

INSIDER TIP:

"I really don't like seeing contact forms without also having a really easy way to email the photographer. The contact form is fine as long as I can copy and paste an email address or click a link to take me directly to the email draft."

— KELLY ELAINE GARTHWAITE, FOUNDER AT HEY Y'ALL!

WHAT NOW?

Now that you know how to introduce yourself and make a strong first impression, it's time to pitch your work to your dream clients. In Chapter 3, we dive into the world of marketing and how to craft the perfect pitch to capture your dream client's attention.

If you've been sending email after email with no response, this chapter is for you. We'll hear from agents, photo editors, and other industry professionals on what captures their attention in an email—and what doesn't. Chances are, it's not you... It's your approach.

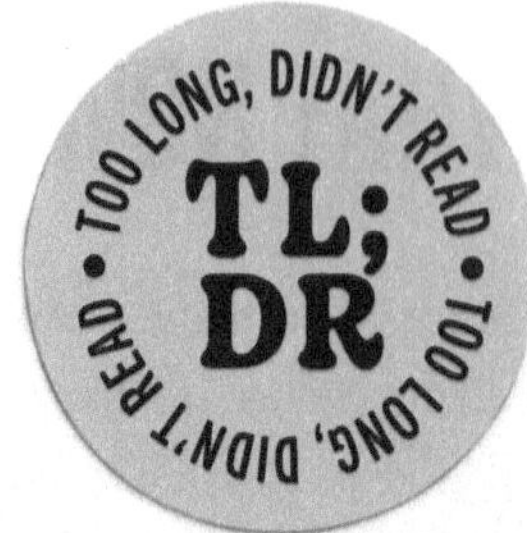

- Presentation is *everything*. Show up as your best self online and in person.

- Build an authentic brand that reflects who you are!

- Find your "secret sauce." It will set you apart from the competition.

- Don't know your niche? Research, explore, and don't be afraid to try new things.

- Your website is your business card — Keep It Simple, Stupid!

- Curate your portfolio to speak directly to your dream clients.

- Ensure fast load times and high-resolution images on your site.

- For the love of all things holy, tell us where you're located!

- Make contacting you easy! Share your email — ditch the forms.

- Remember: you can have the perfect website and still not land the job. You still *need* the talent to back it up!

CHAPTER 3

Marketing: It's Not YOU, It's Them

"Marketing is a long game.
Utilizing it well can keep you top of mind
for when the right jobs come along."

—BLACK VISUAL QUEEN

I see you. You're out there hustling day in and day out—sending emails, honing your craft, asking for portfolio reviews, and trying to connect with industry executives over coffee, often with no response. If you're over it, your frustration is valid. But know this—it's not you, it's them.

Marketing isn't one-size-fits-all. You can craft a flawless email pitch and *still* not get a reply. Here's why: creative executives receive *hundreds* of emails every day from photographers just like you. Trust me, it's overwhelming, and we simply don't have the resources to respond to everyone. Don't get discouraged if you don't hear back right away. Sometimes, we'll look at the email, click on the link, and if the work stands out, we'll bookmark it. If we don't get back to you, it's okay to reach out again in a few weeks. When the right story comes along, your style might be the perfect match, and because you sent a great email pitch, you're going to be top of mind. Now, we're the ones reaching out to you!

INSIDER TIP:

"Whether it's an email, social media, a promo, or a chance meeting, you cannot expect the person to respond immediately or at all. I know that sucks to hear, but it's not possible to respond to every person that contacts us. That doesn't mean we didn't look at what you sent. Just keep at it with a twice-a-year or quarterly cadence, and hopefully, it will pan out. I have kept people I love bookmarked for years before the opportunity came up to work with them. That's how it goes."

— AMY FEITELBERG, FREELANCE PHOTO DIRECTOR AND PRODUCER

MARKETING IS A LONG GAME

One of the toughest parts of freelance photography is getting in front of the right people. You've got to hustle, build your platform, and "play the game," all while keeping up with projects and honing your skills. You want to "be found," but those Cinderella stories are rare without putting in the work. That's exactly why I call it the "photo hustle."

Francesca Galesi, director of photography for AtEdge, sees marketing as more than just a tool—it's a pathway to achieving your goals:

> In today's saturated market, making yourself visible is crucial. With the constant barrage of information in people's lives, effectively marketing and promoting your unique brand is essential. To stand out and attract new leads and clients, you need to use a variety of engaging marketing strategies. I believe that to be found, you must be seen. By utilizing multiple channels and creating personal and compelling content, you can cut through the noise and connect with your creative audience.

She's right. Marketing is a *long* game—a marathon, not a sprint. Try everything until something sticks. But what clicks with one agent or executive may not click with another. Sending email pitches, building a strong newsletter following, updating your website regularly, sending out mailers, and growing a strong platform on social media will all help get you noticed. Industry pros and potential clients are constantly searching for new talent—but you need to make it easy for them to find you, and that's where having a strong social media presence comes into play.

Dear Carly,

I love your work at *Plant Life* magazine focusing on seasonal flora! I'm connected with a local designer whose latest collection was made with illustrated patterns of our region's seasonal plants, and I think it would make a great Spring cover story! Our last collaboration can be viewed here.

Let me know when we can set up a quick fifteen-minute chat.

Melody Alfaro

www.photowebsite.com

SEND

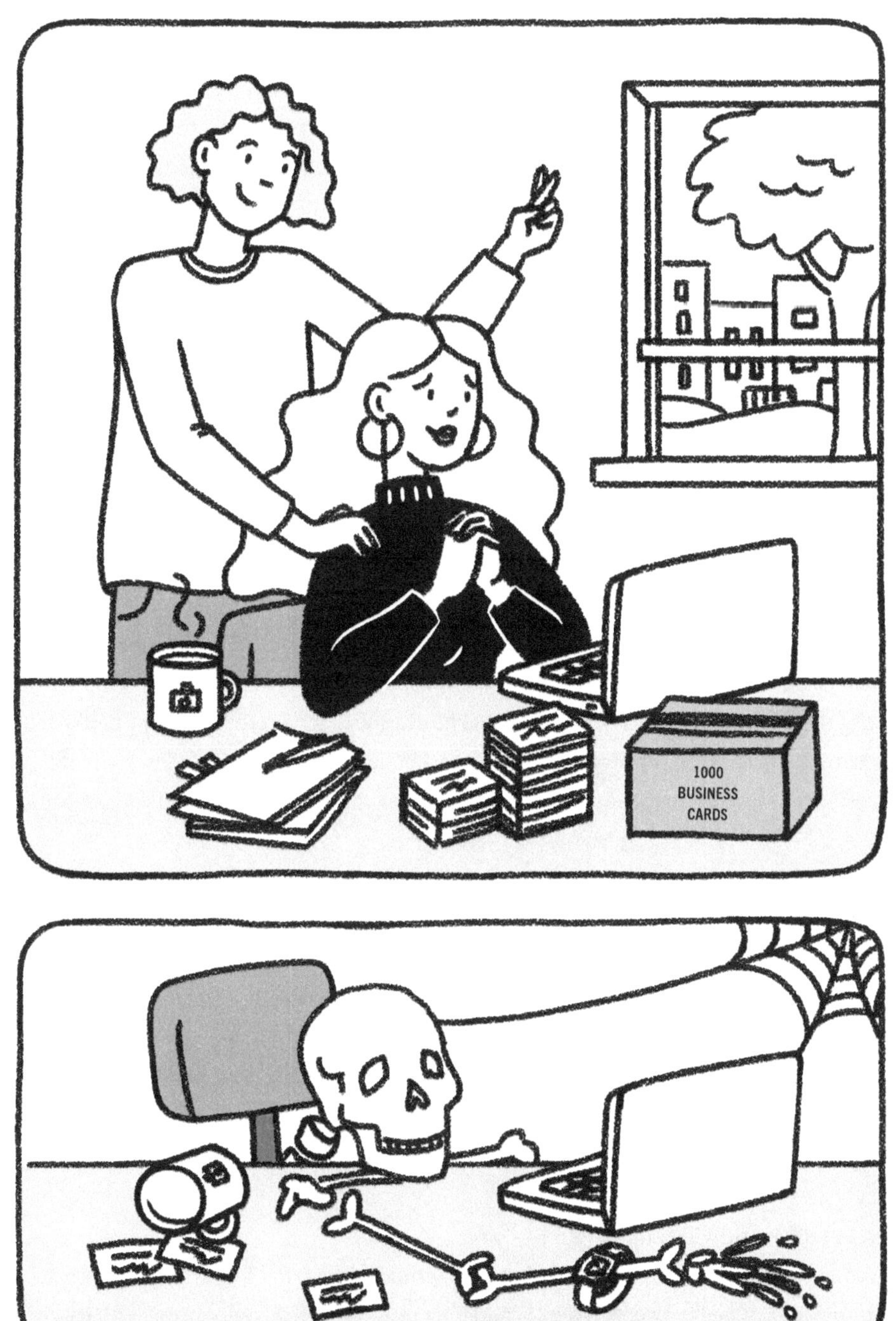
1000
BUSINESS
CARDS

SOCIAL MEDIA PLATFORMS FOR PHOTOGRAPHERS

First off, your website is your home base, so make sure it has everything we need: a beautifully curated portfolio targeting your ideal clients, up-to-date contact information, email, and location. Also, link to all your active social media platforms—and triple-check that these links work.

One of the first things we check is your social media. I've seen websites with broken links or links to private Instagram accounts, which wastes time and causes you to miss opportunities. We want to see your recent work and whether you're consistently sharing the type of imagery you're known for.

Now, let's take a look at the major social media platforms photographers are using to showcase their work.

Instagram

Instagram is the ride-or-die, OG platform for photographers. It remains a top social platform for photographers due to its focus on imagery.

A common question I often get from photographers is whether to separate their business and personal accounts. I've seen both approaches work. Some photographers treat their account as a mix of personal and professional, while others prefer a dedicated, business-only profile. If your account has a mix of both, just keep in mind that clients often check Instagram to see if your feed aligns with the work displayed on your website.

Pinterest

This might surprise you, but Pinterest can be a powerful platform for photographers. Not only is it inspiring, but it can also drive traffic to your website. If someone discovers your black-and-white portraits on Pinterest, clicks on an image, and ends up exploring more, you can guide them back to your website (if you're savvy). Just make sure the images on your site align with the photos on Pinterest. The last thing you want is a beautiful shot on Pinterest that doesn't match the rest of your work or branding. Consistency is key across all platforms!

X, BlueSky, and Threads

Another place photographers hang out is X (formally known as Twitter) along with its alternatives, BlueSky and Threads. While they're all word-focused, you can still catch an editor's attention with the right message. Again, make sure your content (message) is consistent with your brand.

LinkedIn

LinkedIn has gained traction since 2020, offering a place to share behind-the-scenes content, personal growth, and business wins. I love following photographers on this platform because I get a more personal look at their work and business and get to know them on a deeper level. Many companies use this platform to discover new talent.

YouTube and TikTok are also valuable platforms for photographers to showcase their work.

You don't need to use every single platform to succeed—just pick the ones that work best for you. The goal is to make it easy for companies and future clients to find you. For me, it's LinkedIn, Instagram, and Pinterest, but you do *you*! Do your research and experiment with different platforms to find what works for you, and make sure you're staying on top of the algorithms. Don't put all your eggs in one basket, either. There will come a time when that platform comes to an end, so you want to make sure you have your own digital space to fall back on.

Whatever you choose, make sure your website is on point. Be unique and differentiate yourself. There's no magic number to how many emails you need to send before you get a response, how many portfolio reviews you need to have, or how many meetups you need to attend before landing your dream gig—just keep pushing forward.

INSIDER TIP:

"If I see an image that catches my eye in a magazine, at a gallery, in the newspaper, on Instagram, TikTok...anywhere, I will look up that photographer's name to view their work. I also see promos, do portfolio reviews, look at agencies, collectives, books, and on and on."

— AMY FEITELBERG, FREELANCE PHOTO DIRECTOR AND PRODUCER

INSIDER TIP:

"One photographer did this series in a seedy motel room and then shot all different scenes that took place there: a murder, a honeymoon, a prom night party, etc. All on one set and super creative. That really stood out, and we worked a lot together for years after that. Use your imagination, go wild, and have fun. If you do, then so will everyone else."

— GREG GARRY, PHOTO CREATIVE DIRECTOR AND PRODUCER

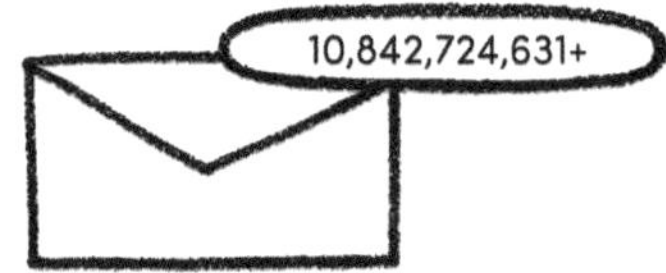

HOW TO SLIDE INTO THE INBOX

I want to focus on email pitches. How you reach out is crucial—you *have* to be strategic. We skim hundreds of emails a day, so you need to figure out a way to grab our attention. What will make us *want* to read your email instead of skimming? What will make us *want* to click on your website? Here's what won't work: a generic email addressed to "Sir or Ma'am" with no real reason to engage. Customize your email for the person you're reaching out to—it shows you did your homework and leaves a lasting impression.

This is exactly why it's so important to *nail* your pitch. Generic, cold-email pitches get deleted, sent to spam, or tossed straight into the trash. The higher up the person is, the busier they are, and they don't have time for impersonal emails. That's why you *have* to be strategic.

Before you send your email, you've got to do your research. People change positions or get laid off, and a message or email that doesn't reflect that gets deleted *immediately.* There's no room for assumptions in a climate where photo and creative departments are shrinking.

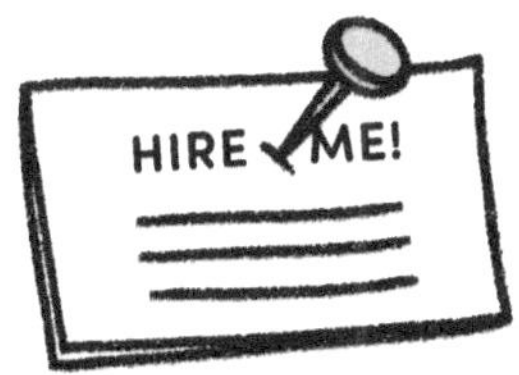

NAILING THE PITCH

When pitching, you're not just saying, "Hey, give me a job." It's about making a connection. Instead, it's more like: "Hey, I'm out here in the world. Here's some recent work I've done. I think it fits with your brand or publication and the work you're producing." Keep it short and sweet, and let your work speak for itself.

Remember, we skim emails in seconds, then head straight to your website. If it grabs my attention, I'll head back to your email to read more. If it's not a good fit for the brand, the publication, or the project, or I can't refer you to a colleague, it's deleted.

Before sending your pitch, make sure:

1. Your presentation is on point.

2. Your website showcases your best work and speaks the language of the publication or brand you're reaching out to.

3. You've done your research on the company or publication and know exactly who you're reaching out to and what they do.

Now you're ready to pitch, but first, let's take a look at a bad pitch (the kind that goes straight to the garbage).

Here's an example of a bad pitch that goes straight to the trash:

Dear Sir/Ma'am.

I'm a pet photographer in Florida. I would love to work with you.
Here's a link to my website.

Signature

If I click on your website and it's just okay—more lifestyle than high-fashion and not aligned with my publication—it leaves me wondering why you pitched me in the first place. Delete.

Now, here's an example of a good pitch that will get my attention:

Let's say I work at a high-fashion magazine and receive this cold pitch from a photographer.

Dear Karen,

I loved your publication's retrospective of Taylor Swift's cats. I'm a pet photographer based in Florida, and there's a booming scene here of CEO housewives who have their own going-out squad, complete with amazing poodles in matching outfits. I have attached some samples and would love to discuss featuring this project in your next issue or on your website.

Let me know when we can set up a quick fifteen-minute chat.

Signature

Link to website.

Now, let me ask you: which email would get your attention? The first is generic and lacks a clear call to action. The second shows they've done their research, referenced a relevant story, and pitched a unique angle with a simple next step.

Remember: if you're pitching us, we will have to pitch you to the editorial team. They'll ask the same questions we want the answers to in your pitch—who, what, when, where, and why. Why is this important, and how is your work different? Make sure your pitch stands out. If it's not unique, why should we care? It's all about the long game—you'll win some and you'll lose some. In the long run, the more specific and standout the pitch, the more successful you'll be.

Let's look at a sample email template:

Subject: Your subject line needs to be clear and concise, informing the recipient about the nature of the email and who it is from.

Greeting: Address the recipient by name to make the email more personal.

Body of Message: Start with a polite introduction that states your purpose for writing and identifies your area of photographic specialization.

Mention your experience and suggest a compatibility between your photographic style and the company's or publication's aesthetic. You can also show that you're familiar with their work and that there's a synergy between your respective goals and values.

Include a direct link to your professional portfolio where the recipient can view your work.

Close the email with gratitude and express eagerness about any future prospects.

INSIDER TIP:

"You have to reach out! While I believe in implementing a strategic marketing plan with trackable goals and stats, you can't let that undertaking get in the way of simply starting. The most basic marketing tool you have is connecting with potential clients. Do your research, be thoughtful with your message, always include an image or e-card (linked to your website) in the body of your email and have a signature with your contact information. Contact that person every time you have new work to share. Stay top of mind."

— JENNIFER PERLMUTTER, SENIOR PHOTO AND MOTION REPRESENTATIVE

HOW TO SET UP A MEETING (AND WHAT TO DO WHEN YOU GET THERE)

Every single email pitch should include a clear call to action. One of my favorites is to request a fifteen- to thirty-minute meeting to discuss your work. With tools like Zoom, Google Meet, or Microsoft Teams, it's really easy to jump on a call with someone no matter their location. And if they're local, a remote meeting may still be a great option if their schedule is full.

If you're in the same city, you can offer to meet in person, especially if you're visiting town. If the person declines, follow up with, "Thank you for your time. Let me know when you have time to meet in the future. By the way, would you like to be added to my newsletter?" This keeps the door open for future connections. Remember, the strategy with marketing is to always stay top of mind and always keep the door open.

Let's say your email pitch landed you a meeting—what now? You need to come prepared. The same goes for portfolio reviews. Here are a few pointers to ensure your meeting goes smoothly:

1. **Be early.**

Remember, people are busy, and if they're squeezing you in between meetings, time is limited. Being early shows respect for their schedule.

2. **State your intention for the meeting.**

Share your goals for the meeting with them before you ever get face-to-face. People aren't mind readers—let them know what you want to discuss via email or after you've said your hellos.

3. **Prepare questions in advance.**

Don't expect the other person to carry the meeting—that's your responsibility. Prepare a few questions to ask and let the conversation flow organically. Bonus points if your questions reflect research into the person and their past work.

4. **Be professional and confident.**

Your confidence in your work and professionalism will leave a lasting impression— make it a positive one.

5. **Be aware of time.**

Set a timer five minutes before you're supposed to end the meeting and start wrapping up. Again, people are busy, and it's crucial to respect the time they give you.

6. Be grateful.

This should go without saying, but I'm going to say it: be polite and show gratitude for the meeting. This goes a long way—trust me.

Not every meetup will result in a job on the spot. The person you meet with may still need to pitch you to their editorial team. Remember: you have to be the right fit for the job. Be patient and trust the process. If the meeting went well and they like your work, you'll be top of mind for future opportunities that match your niche and the company or brand's visual guidelines.

By now, the hustle really feels like hustle, doesn't it? If you're a photographer who loves shooting but doesn't enjoy the business side, you might be wondering if an agent could help manage those aspects. Let's find out.

WHAT'S AN AGENT, AND DO I NEED ONE?

An agent helps open doors to more work and represents you to clients, acting as a middleperson, similar to a literary agent for authors. They market you to their networks and take a commission from the jobs they secure. Many established (and fully booked) photographers use agents to manage their workload and the heavy lifting of marketing.

Agents help photographers by:

- Opening doors and establishing relationships
- Landing you meetings
- Handling your email marketing
- Building and maintaining your website
- Handling all contracts and negotiations when you get a gig
- Providing legal expertise

Basically, a good agent handles everything but the shoot, letting you focus on your creative work. Agents allow you to concentrate on what you love and less on what you don't.

DO I *NEED* AN AGENT?

I will be the first to tell you that you don't *need* an agent to get work, especially if you're just starting out. Eventually, it's a choice only you can make. Agents earn a commission, so if you're not yet booking a lot of jobs, that expense may not fit your budget—and that's okay. I asked my colleagues if they believe photographers need an agent in this current landscape. Greg Garry, a photo creative director and producer, says, "They [agents] aren't the saviors they promise to be. They do help established photographers keep track of their work and billing, but these days, the shooter really has to be their own advocate."

Many colleagues agree that agents aren't essential for editorial work, where negotiations and contracts are simpler than brand gigs. Kelly Garthwaite, founder of Hey Y'all!, shares that it's really case-by-case:

> I know plenty of photographers who are doing *great* without an agent and others who have an agent but haven't noticed a major difference in the amount of work they are getting since signing on with theirs. Having an agent can be great, but it's not necessarily a cure-all for a photographer's career success.

Jen Jenkins, founder of Giant Artists, adds that agents can be valuable partners for photographers looking to develop long-term careers.

INSIDER TIP:

"It *is* easier to work with an agent on a commercial job, but if we love the photographer's work, it's not going to stop that person from being hired. If they don't have an agent and they are getting a commercial job, they can maybe consult or do an ad hoc thing with an agent, and that helps. In cases of commercial work, I want the agent to protect the photographer. It's not about getting the most amount of money out of the situation, it's about knowing what to ask for, so no one feels exploited at the end of the deal. But again, I would still hire someone without one."

— AMY FEITELBERG, FREELANCE PHOTO DIRECTOR AND PRODUCER

INSIDER TIP:

"We are your business partners, advocates, and cheerleaders. Every rep works a bit differently, but I like to assess and align an artist's creative vision and goals with what truly speaks to their soul. I know that sounds all woo-woo, but it is important that artists are excited about the work they are creating and the people and companies they are creating it with and for. Otherwise, the burnout is real!"

— JENNIFER PERLMUTTER, SENIOR PHOTO AND MOTION REPRESENTATIVE

PROS AND CONS OF WORKING WITH AN AGENT

Agents can be great partners in connecting you with clients, but other times, they can be a total nightmare. Sometimes, an agent's attitude or lack of communication can lead clients to bypass them altogether. There have been many instances where I tried to hire a photographer, only to find out that the agent hadn't even informed them about the project. Now, I often go to photographers directly. If they prefer, I go through their agent instead; I'm more than happy to do that.

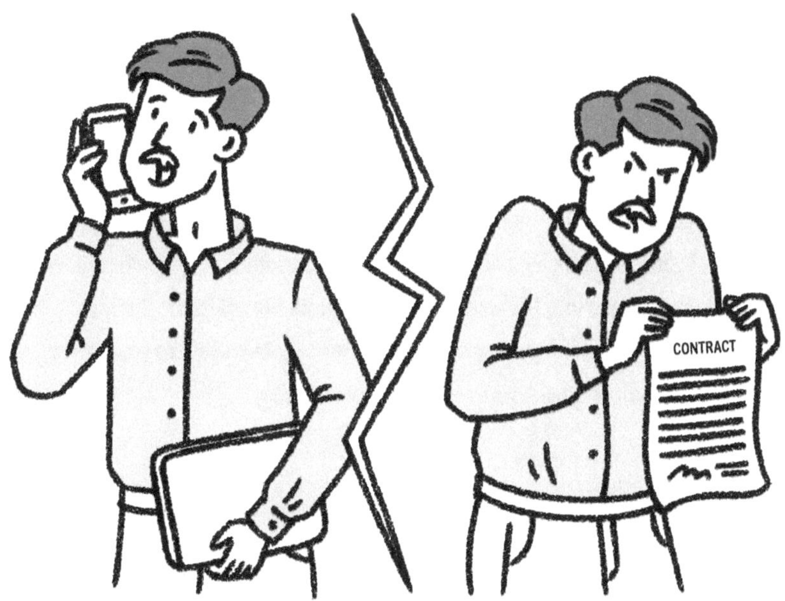

Hear me out, though: not all agents are bad. As with everything else, if you're considering hiring an agent, do your research. Reach out to other photographers about their representation. Are their agents responsive, proactive, and effective at connecting them with the right clients? Do they earn the commission they take? Some photographers have had nightmare experiences after signing contracts with agents who under-deliver and even restrict them from taking on outside work independently. Always *read those contracts before you sign them.* Sometimes, an agent says all the right things until you sign that contract. Then, once you start working together, it's a disaster.

Some photographers only work with agents for brand gigs, where contracts, estimates, negotiations, non-disclosure agreements, and other legal issues can be complex—while handling editorial work themselves. Others manage everything themselves and are happy to do so. There's no right or wrong answer here. It all comes down to what's right for *you.*

INSIDER TIP:

"When I start working with a new artist, I like to build a strategic plan. We assess what we are working with, and year over year, we review our goals to see where we hit the mark and where we need to adjust to drive your business and creative endeavors forward. A photographer and photo agent should, at their best, work in tandem to promote the work to potential clients. Oftentimes, a rep comes to the table with these connections and already knows you would be a good fit for them. It is our job to crack that door open and your job to walk through it. When an inquiry/project comes in, we help facilitate creative calls, introduce you to producers to work with, if needed, help estimate the project, review all contracts to protect your interests, and run all communication with the agency/brand. When that work is released into the world, we shout it from the rooftops! Our most exciting days are when we get to reach out to our clients and share your latest!"

— JENNIFER PERLMUTTER, SENIOR PHOTO AND MOTION REPRESENTATIVE

WHAT AGENTS LOOK FOR IN A PHOTOGRAPHER

It all comes back to presentation. If you're looking for representation, target agencies that align with your niche. Photo agencies usually have a roster of photographers covering different disciplines. As you're doing your research, ask yourself: Is your work as strong as, or stronger than, what's on their site? What sets you apart, and how do you fit in? Agencies usually focus on a specific niche—whether it's hair and makeup, high fashion, lifestyle, food, or something else. They're looking for photographers who fit their aesthetic and can enhance their current lineup. So, think about why they should bring *you* on.

Remember: an agent's main goal is making money. They add photographers to their agencies who are commercially viable for big-budget productions, which means they may be more risk-averse to taking on emerging photographers without a solid track record. The photographers working with agents are well-established and getting enough work to justify paying someone a commission. Keep in mind that what works financially for one photographer may not work for you. And that's okay!

Agents are looking for driven photographers who understand the hustle it takes to build a career. Jen Jenkins, founder of Giant Artists, notes that the agent/photographer relationship is actually more of a partnership; she looks for photographers who are "actively doing the work needed to produce a strong career... Photographers who are making it happen and not waiting for it to happen to them." Other traits valued by Jenkins and other agents include consistency, versatility across both brand and editorial, self-motivation, and teamwork.

The good news? These are skills you can learn and develop! If you're aiming for agent representation, keep honing your craft, keep hustling, and keep growing your skills.

BUILDING YOUR NETWORK

If you want *in*, networking is essential—it's often about who you know and who can introduce you to the right people. If your network is limited, it's time to get proactive. Use LinkedIn, hit up your friends, and tap into your connections. Visit magazine racks, note the mastheads of the publications you admire, and search for email contacts to start making genuine connections that could lead to future opportunities.

Networking means asking for portfolio reviews, meeting other industry creatives for coffee, and engaging in meaningful exchanges. Networking is a give-and-take process. It's not just about asking for introductions; it's about offering value. Consider how you can support others in their projects. This mutual support builds lasting relationships, keeps you top of mind for future projects, and often results in referrals.

For example, if you're at a networking event or creative mixer and you meet a hairstylist or makeup artist, initiate a conversation and stay in touch. Maybe you can collaborate on a test shoot, allowing you both to build your portfolios—a win-win!

Now that we've covered self-promotion, photo agents, and networking, it's time to talk about who's actually in the room, who you should be reaching out to, and the dos and don'ts of asking for introductions.

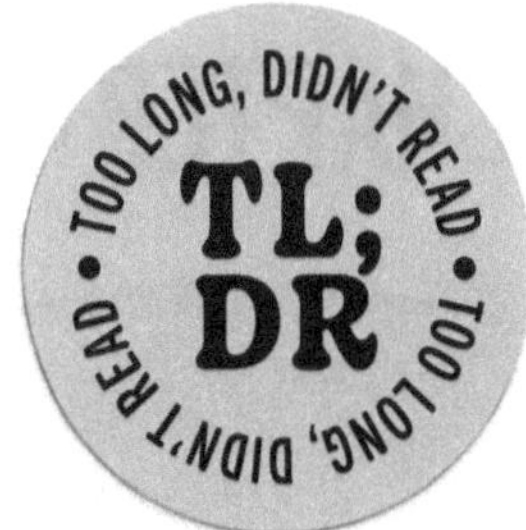

- Marketing is a long game.

- Strong referrals are the best form of marketing.

- What works for one person may not work for another.
  Try everything!

- Don't be afraid to stand out by being unique and authentic.

- Thoughtful outreach is essential. Strategy matters!

- Do not (I repeat, do not) send generic emails.
  Those will go straight to the trash!

- Do your research and craft personalized, targeted pitches.

- Don't forget to include a clear call to action.
  What do you want us to do with your email?

- You don't *need* a photo agent, but they can be helpful for brand deals.

- This business is all about who you know.
  Building your network is crucial!

CHAPTER 4

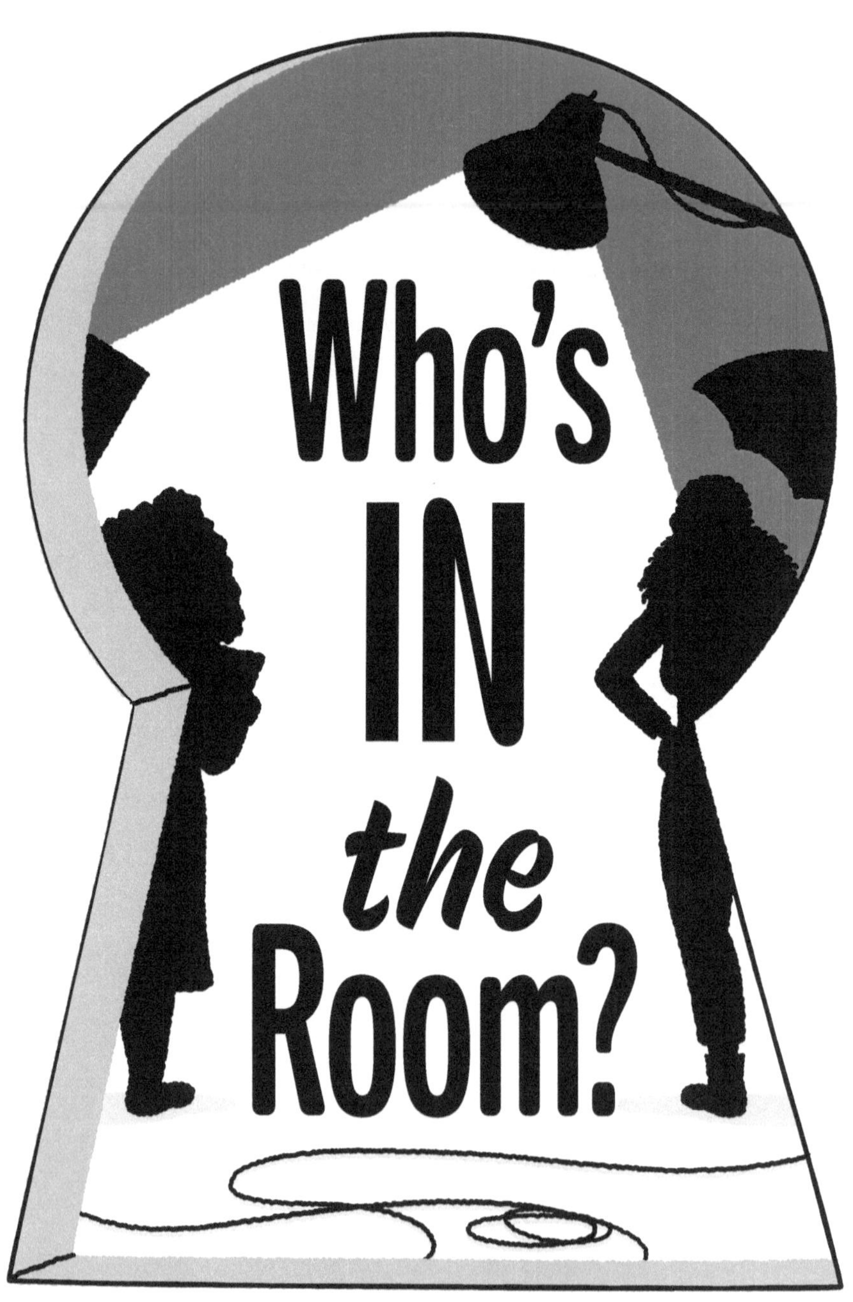

> "Always do your research on who's in the room.
> Know who you're working with!"
>
> —BLACK VISUAL QUEEN

My career almost ended before it ever began.

On my first day in publishing, I made a *huge* rookie mistake—one that could have cost me my entire career. I was very green. I didn't know much about publishing at this point, apart from the little experience I'd had during my post-college internship. During my orientation, the executive assistant introduced me to the staff: "the people in the room." I remember walking into one office and meeting this guy. I had no idea who he was, and I almost asked, "Who are you, and what do you do here?" Luckily, the assistant quickly stepped in and introduced him as the editor-in-chief.

Oh my gosh, she *saved* my life! I was mortified. I hadn't done my research. I had not looked at the masthead, and I clearly had no idea who the key players were! This is why it's critical to do your research and *know who's who*—before you ever step foot into the building.

This reminds me of a scene in the movie *The Devil Wears Prada*. I give you permission to put this book down right now and go watch it. Think of it as part of your research. And if you haven't seen it, I'm going to spoil the first part for you.

There's a scene where Andrea Sachs (played by Anne Hathaway) walks into the offices of *Runway Magazine* for an interview to be the editor-in-chief's personal assistant. As she's getting briefed by an overly stressed-out woman named Emily (Emily Blunt's character), she asks, "Who's Miranda?" to which Emily responds, "Oh my god, I will pretend you did not just ask that. She's the editor-in-chief of *Runway* ... not to mention, a legend!"[3]

Listen up, people: that was almost me, so do your research! Knowing who's who isn't just about avoiding embarrassment; it shows respect and makes a good first impression. So, before you send an email, before you walk onto a set for the very first time, know who will be there, what their names are, and their roles. This includes knowing the editor-in-chief, the director of photography, the creative director, down to the photo assistant and researcher. Each role contributes to the project, and knowing their names and what they do there shows that you're informed and prepared.

Don't worry. I'm about to give you a crash course. Let me walk you through who is on set, what they do, and why they're in the room. But first, a disclaimer: not every publication or brand uses the same job titles—a director of photography might be a photo director elsewhere, and a photo researcher at one publication might be the equivalent to the art buyer at another brand. Write these down if you need to, but whatever you do, don't skip the research!

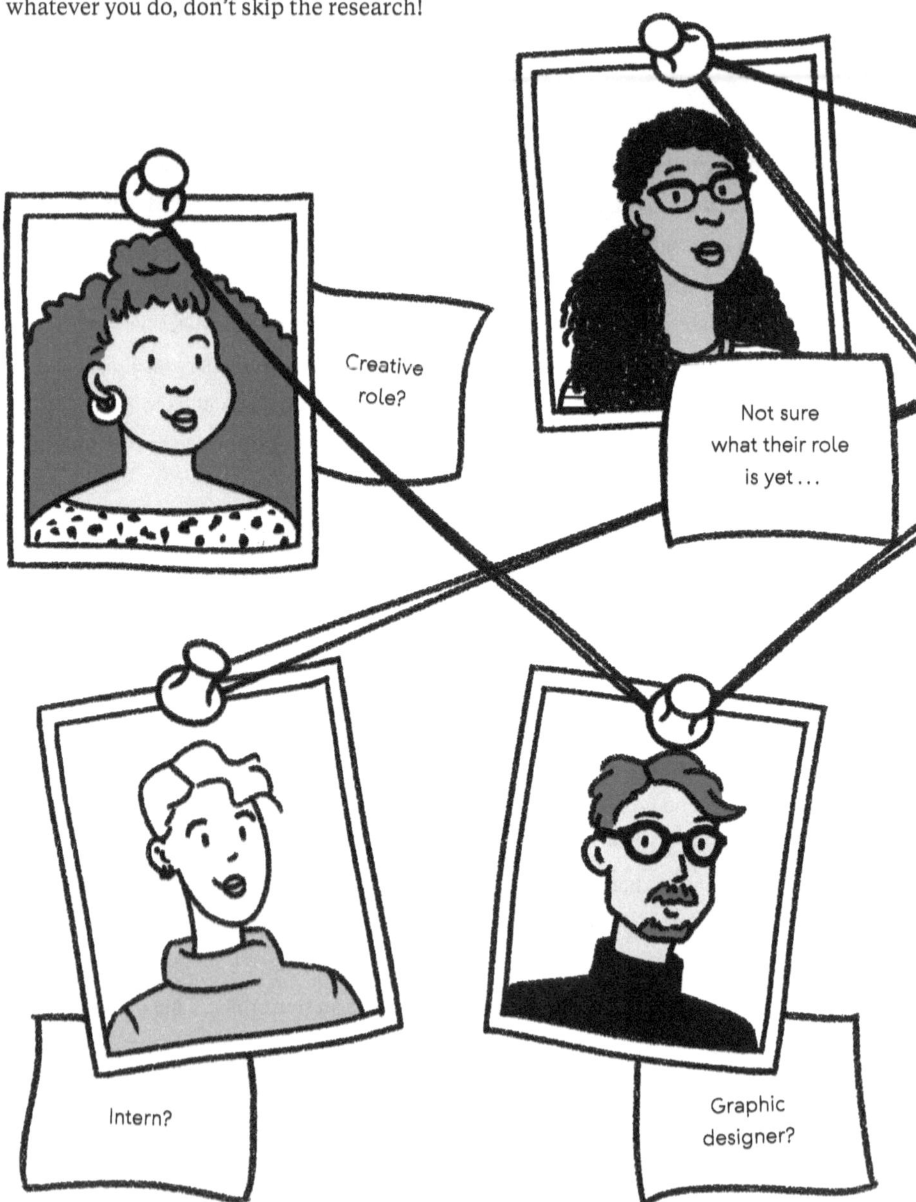

WHO'S ON THE MASTHEAD?

Here's a breakdown of a magazine or editorial masthead structure. Keep in mind that in branding, advertising, and tech, these roles are often labeled differently. In the brand world, these mastheads are called "org charts." While an editor-in-chief may not exist in brand or tech spaces, similar roles, like creative, art, or design directors, serve similar purposes.

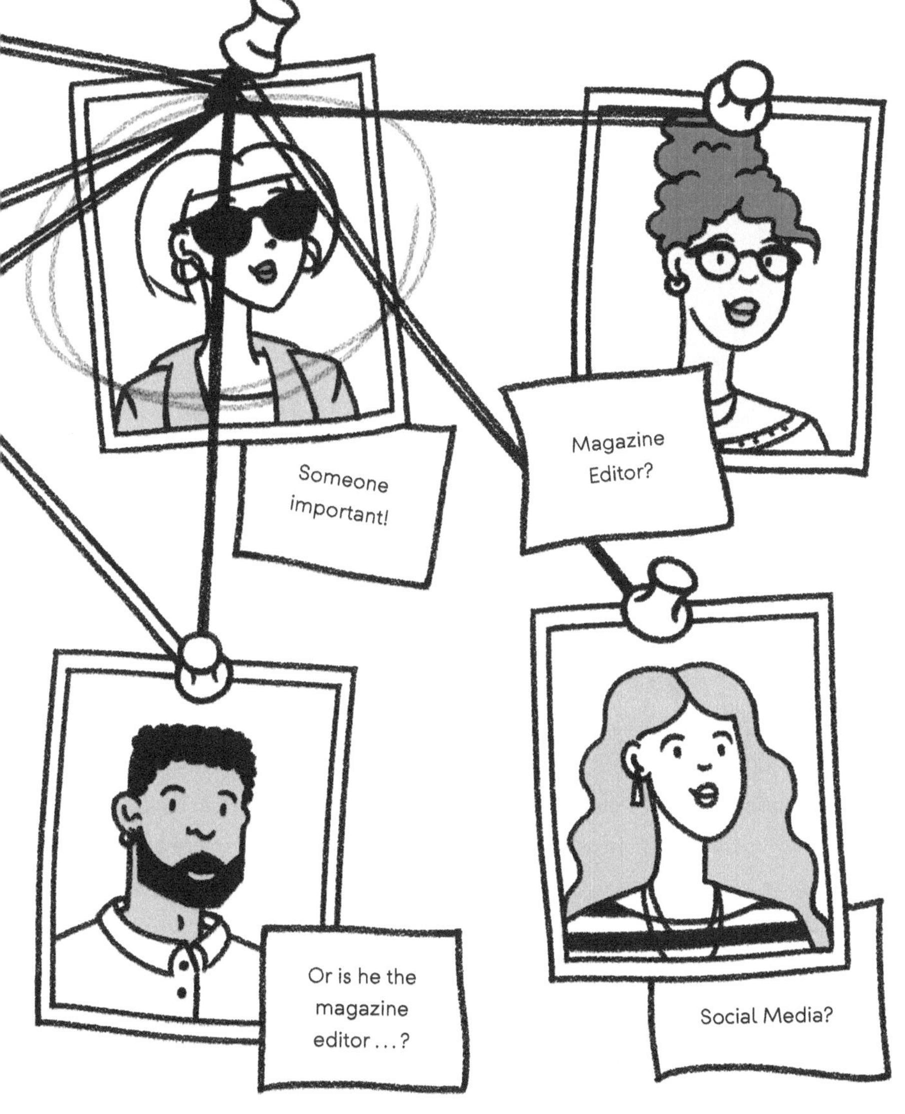

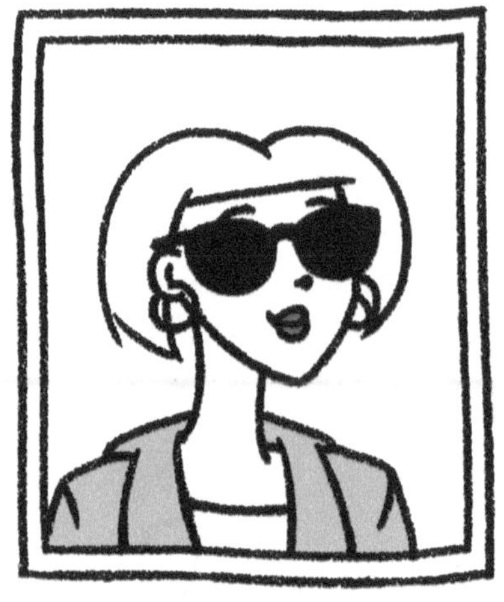

Editor-in-Chief

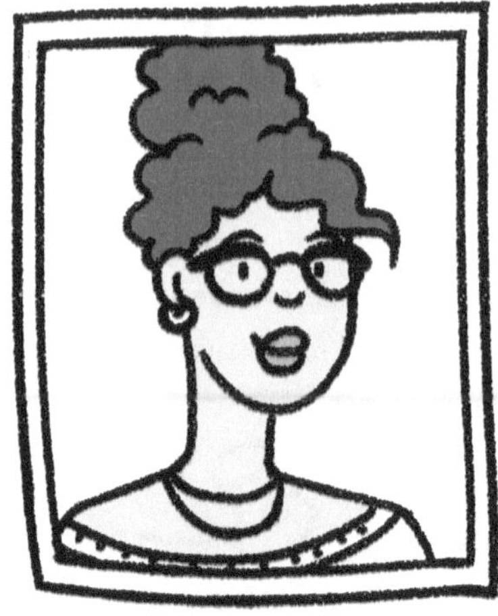

Managing Editor

LEADERSHIP AND EDITORIAL DEPARTMENT:

- **Editor-in-Chief (EIC):** The top executive and head decision-maker responsible for the entire publication's vision, brand, and staff, who oversees design, layout, and content. They make final decisions on cover choices, layout, and overall direction. Think of them as the vision keepers—like Anna Wintour at *Vogue*, the Miranda Priestly character from *The Devil Wears Prada*, or Nina Garcia of *Elle*. They protect the brand image and guide every team to align with the publication's goals.

- **Managing Editor:** This person handles the day-to-day operations, managing workflows, scheduling deadlines, and serving as the bridge between the editorial departments and the EIC, ensuring everything runs smoothly and on time.[4]

- **Executive Editor:** Often second in command to the EIC, the executive editor focuses on developing editorial strategies, managing special projects, and overseeing specific sections of the publication.[5]

- **Senior Editor:** Reporting to the executive editor, the senior editor oversees specific sections of the publication and manages a team of writers and editors dedicated to specific areas of content.[6]

- **Features Editor:** Responsible for the publication's features section, this editor pitches ideas, commissions articles, and works closely with writers and freelancers to develop in-depth, engaging content.

- **Associate Editor:** Handles smaller sections and assists senior editors with various tasks to support the editorial team.
- **Assistant Editor:** Primarily works on story development, handling tasks like researching, fact-checking, editing, and some writing.
- **Staff Writer/Reporter:** Responsible for writing articles and reports. Many publications also outsource this role to freelancers.
- **Copy Editor:** Most publications have at least one copy editor. This person reviews and corrects the copy for grammatical errors and typos, and ensures the content follows brand guidelines.
- **Fact Checker:** It costs publications money and time (and a bit of pride) to submit a redaction or correction for a story. This person ensures the accuracy of content by verifying facts, sources, and citations to prevent errors.

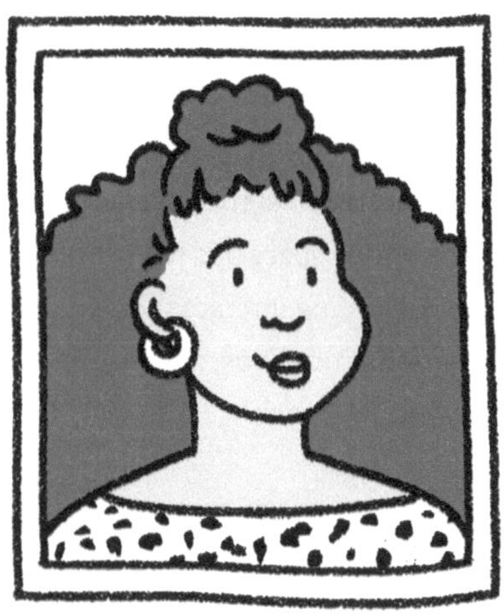

Creative Director

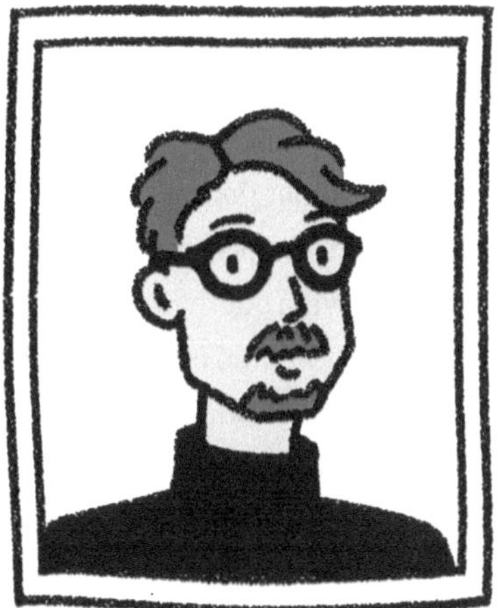

Design Director

ART/CREATIVE DEPARTMENT:

- **Creative Director:** Head of the creative department, shaping the visual direction of the publication. They collaborate with the EIC or the chief marketing officer to ensure the brand vision and tone are maintained. The creative director oversees the design and photo teams, managing both the creative ideas and strategic execution to uphold the brand's integrity.[7]
- **Design Director:** Manages the design department's day-to-day operations

and acts as a liaison between design and other departments to ensure the creative director's vision is implemented. They handle the budget, supervise supporting staff, and focus on the design and visual storytelling of the features or campaigns of the brand or publication.[8]

• **Senior Art Director:** This person is a senior-level leader who oversees all aspects of the brand campaign or editorial publication. They provide creative art direction for designers, photographers, and illustrators while managing stories, developing concepts, and leading the team. They also take the lead on higher-profile projects and stories.

• **Art Director:** If not the sole director, this person helps support the senior art director by carrying out their vision for the publication or brand campaign. This position would be working to implement the vision given by the senior art director while overseeing the visuals of campaigns, creating designs and layouts, and helping manage the front and back sections of a publication.

• **Associate Art Director:** Assists the senior art director and art director with design tasks and administrative duties. They support smaller projects and stories, helping with design and other needs as required.

• **Art Assistant:** Supports the art department, designers, and leaders by handling administrative tasks, scheduling meetings, running errands, and assisting with creative needs to keep projects on track.

• **Graphic Designer:** Designs the graphics for brand campaigns, stories, websites, and other visual content. This specialized role focuses on creating visually appealing designs to meet the brand's needs.

• **Layout Artist:** Combines the designs and content, ensuring there's plenty of balance, white space, and composition on every page of the magazine or website.[9]

• **Interactive Designer:** Works primarily in the online space of a publication or brand, creating interactive or animated illustrations, designs, and text for websites or stories.[10]

Many publications also have production or operations teams that manage the physical product or execution of the publication or campaign. These roles can include production managers, operations managers, and project managers. Additionally, there are often digital or web-based media teams, social media teams, and video teams.

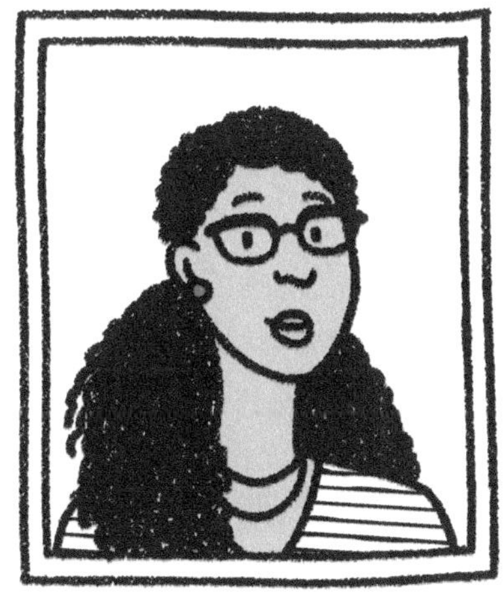

Photo Director

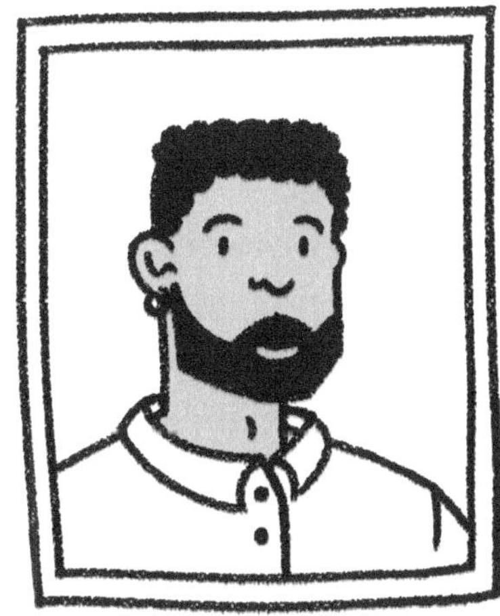

Photo Editor

♡ PHOTO DEPARTMENT:

- **Director of Photography or Photo Director:** Oversees the entire photo department, guiding the vision of the publication, brand, or campaign. They uphold the quality and style of the visuals for the publication or brand while also handling the logistics of budgets and planning. This person collaborates with the creative director, design department, managing editor, and EIC for a successful project or outcome.

- **Associate Photo Director (or Associate Director of Photography):** This person acts as the managing editor for the brand or publication. If this role doesn't exist, these duties typically fall to the senior photo editor or photo editor.

- **Senior Photo Editor:** Manages the day-to-day operations and works with the director of photography to create visuals for the magazine. They tackle assignments and work on covers, main features, celebrities, and major stories.

- **Photo Editor:** Works on visuals for stories for the brand or publication, handling everything from photo selection and editing to layout and positioning within articles. They also commission photographers, negotiate rates, and manage contracts. In branding, this role may be called a photo art director, photo lead, photo campaign manager, or photo producer. Photo editors often juggle multiple tasks and are essential to making projects come together—especially in today's world of lean staff. They are the unsung heroes of "getting it done." This job can *break* you. It can burn you out.

You will either love it or hate it... There is no in-between. It's a demanding role, but for those passionate about it, it can be incredibly rewarding.

• **Associate or Assistant Photo Editor:** Handles many of the same tasks as the photo editor, but often on a smaller scale. They may focus on the front and back of the books or publications. They manage administrative duties, photo research, permissions, and rights management as well.

• **Photo Assistant:** Provides administrative support, assists with photo research, and helps the photo team with various tasks as needed.

• **Staff Photographer:** An in-house photographer tasked with shooting most of the visuals for the magazine or publication. Due to the scale of work, some projects may be outsourced to freelancers. This role is becoming increasingly rare.

• **Photo Producer:** The photo producer is a logistical all-star. They make sure everyone is taken care of, handling photo releases, locations, scouting, transportation, *everything*. This role involves knowing all the ins and outs, all the rules and regulations, and the tiniest details to prevent any hiccups. Producers handle logistics, contracts, legalities, payments, and invoicing, and keep the project moving seamlessly.

• **DigiTech (Digital Imaging Technician):** Responsible for photo file naming, color profile accuracy, and organization, the DigiTech ensures that photo files are accessible and secure. They're the unsung heroes of all shoots, often saving the day by backing up all files to prevent data loss if something goes wrong.

• **Photo Researcher:** Responsible for sourcing all images needed for a publication or brand. This role involves working with stock and publicity agencies, securing photo and illustration licenses, and finding specific images to support stories. Whether it's building a timeline of a celebrity relationship or sourcing rare archival shots, a photo researcher lives and breathes image curation—it's all they do.[11]

A NOTE FROM KAREN:

These days, it's very rare to have an in-house photographer on staff. When I started out, there were stories about how crowded the offices used to be—until 2012, when they had six staff photographers. By the following January, budget cuts halved that number. It was a bloodbath. For larger brands, it's often cheaper to hire freelancers than to pay someone a salary plus benefits.

Remember: I'm here to keep it real with you. If your goal is to be a staff photographer, that's great, but know that you'll be asked to shoot everything. You won't count against the budget, which means you'll be double or even triple-booked. One staff photographer I knew even had to take the CEO's passport photo. When I said you get tasked with shooting everything, I meant everything.

I always advise photographers who go the staff route to make sure they truly love the brand. You'll be living and breathing their lookbook, identity, and guidelines. But remember, if you get laid off, your portfolio will only reflect that brand's vision—unless you've been doing personal projects to keep your creativity sharp. I'm not trying to discourage you. I understand the desire for a stable staff role, especially if you've been struggling to find consistent work as a freelancer. But I do want you to walk into that role prepared for what you might experience along the way.

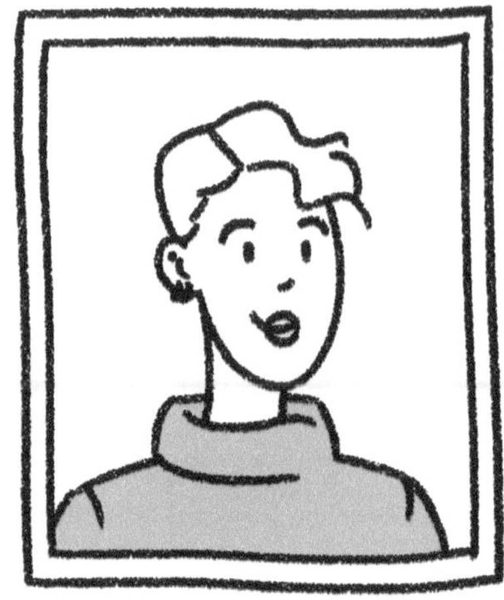

Digital Editor

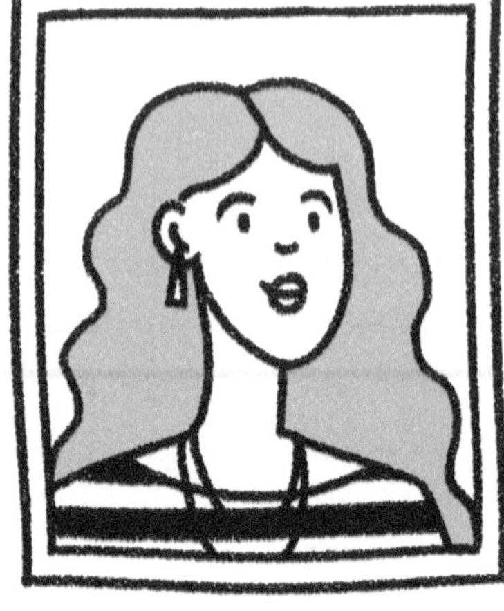

Social Media Manager

DIGITAL MEDIA TEAM:

- **Digital Editor/Online Editor:** Manages the brand or publication's online presence, keeping the website current, working with a team to publish well-written content, and ensuring smooth site functionality. [12]
- **Video Producer:** Creates visual content for the brand or publication, often handling budgets, writing scripts, and overseeing the production process from start to finish.[13]

- **Social Media Manager:** Manages the brand or publication's social media presence, collaborating with content or marketing teams to produce engaging, on-brand content that is published on social media in creative and fun ways, and maintaining the brand's "voice" across platforms. [14]

SEARCH

🔍 Who is the Editor-in-Chief of . . .

DO YOUR DUE DILIGENCE

When researching these positions, keep in mind that staffing changes—layoffs and cut positions—may not be immediately reflected on a publication's mastheads or brand website. Organizational changes often take time to appear online. Why am I telling you this? Because you need to do your research beyond the masthead: look people up, dig deeper, and remember that LinkedIn profiles may not be updated right away. So, if you're getting some bounced emails, it may be that your contact no longer works for that brand or publication.

WHO'S ACTUALLY IN THE ROOM?

Once you know the key roles on a publication's masthead (or company directory), it's essential to know who is typically present during a photoshoot. These are the people that you'll want to reach out to. Remember, doing your research is key. You need to know each position, what their name is, what they do, and why they're in the room. Then...memorize it until you know it like the back of your hand.

- **Editor-in-Chief:** The EIC generally attends high-profile shoots, like covers, celebrity features, or major stories, to oversee and make key decisions. For smaller features or other sections of the publication, they are usually not present.
- **Creative Director:** This person will be in the room more often than the EIC, especially for big feature stories, cover shoots, and other large-budget projects.
- **Art Director:** The art director will likely be present at most photoshoots, providing guidance and vision and ensuring the project stays on track. They play a key role in maintaining the visual consistency of both brand campaigns and publication features.
- **Photo Director:** The photo director is almost always present at shoots, acting as the main point of contact. They work to ensure the shoot runs smoothly and stays within budget, making sure both the creative vision and practical needs are met.

MASTHEADS ARE *SHRINKING*

Before the 2008 recession, company mastheads were full, often listing dozens of positions, especially in the photo department. It wasn't rare for there to be twenty-plus people in it. But since the layoffs of 2008, these departments have dwindled to just one or two people managing all the visual needs for the entire company or publication. Executives now ask, "What is the smallest number of people we can employ to get the job done?" Today, mastheads tend to be editorial-heavy, with lean creative teams handling extensive workloads. Let me tell you—it's no easy task.

Why am I telling you this? Because when you're pitching to editorial publications or brands, it's helpful to understand that most mastheads and company directories are lean, especially the photo departments. Many people juggle multiple roles, making them *extremely* busy. If you don't hear back immediately after pitching, don't take it personally! Chances are, if they like your work, they'll keep your information for future gigs.

OTHER THINGS YOU NEED TO KNOW ABOUT WHO'S IN THE ROOM

Being around talented individuals working toward a common goal can be intimidating, but talent alone won't sustain you. It also requires hard work—and lots of it. That's why you have to take charge of your personal growth and career—network, learn, listen, and stay on top of industry trends. Always be learning new skills, refining old ones, and understanding your craft inside and out. And remember, know the roles of those around you; it's key to building strong working relationships.

Here's an example: I made an effort to learn about writing and design to better understand the language of my coworkers who studied journalism and design in school. This helped me connect with my coworkers, as they saw that I was trying to understand their perspective. My approach was always, "I'm here to help—what do you need from me photo-wise?" To succeed and be a strong team player, we need to meet people where they are and try to understand their roles from their perspective.

Does that mean you need to go to journalism school or get a design degree? Not at all. I took affordable online courses—one was on sale for $49.99!—to learn the basics of design history and the process of putting a layout together. Now, when I'm creating the visuals, I keep the designer's needs in mind and think about how I can best assist them. For example, I might say, "I noticed in your previous design you were going for a certain look; this photo might fit that idea well."

The more I learn, the better I become at my job—and the same goes for you. Keeping your skills sharp and staying curious will also help during lean times. Having a broad skill set and a solid reputation is invaluable. Remember those one-person photo departments? If you're ever running the show, you'll be the essential utility player in the room.

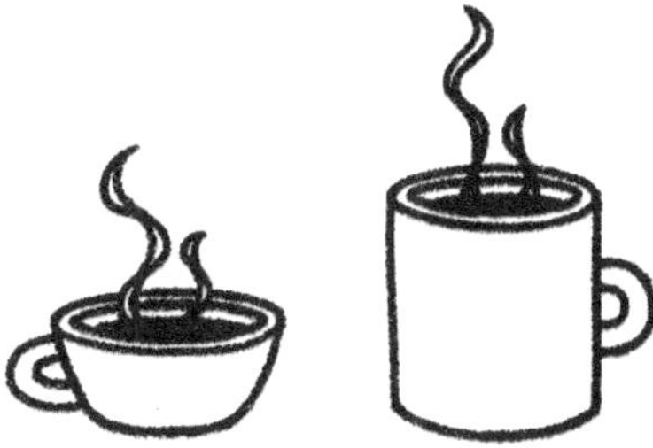

WHO SHOULD I REACH OUT TO?

Start by connecting with the photo editor. Photo departments are often open to fresh talent and new work but may not have the time or bandwidth to respond immediately—especially if you're not currently working together. But that doesn't mean we don't want to work with you. Be patient with us!

After you reach out, follow up a few weeks later. In your pitch, include a clear call to action. Tailor your pitch to each person you contact, making it compelling enough for them to respond—whether it's for coffee, a portfolio review, or a Zoom meetup.

When you're reaching out to senior staff or company executives, it's best to have a prior connection or direct contact first. The higher the rank someone holds in a company, the less time they have, and they often have assistants filtering their emails. That means if you're cold emailing a creative director, you have to *wow* them with your pitch and website; they need to be impressive enough to capture (and keep) their attention.

Disclaimer: Every photo director, editor, producer, creative director, art director, and production company will have unique preferences. Some appreciate printed mailers; others don't. Some prefer face-to-face meetings, while others will reach out only when they need you! Once you're in contact, be sure to ask them directly about their preferred approach.

INSIDER TIPS:

"Utilize your existing network first. See if you can get introductions from someone you already know. Aside from that, it's a numbers game. Do the cold emailing or messaging, but make sure you're doing it in a thoughtful way, where the person you're messaging knows that you've done your research. Put your personality in the messaging. If it's been a few weeks since you sent the first message and you haven't heard back, follow up. Sometimes, a follow-up is really necessary."

— KELLY GARTHWAITE, FOUNDER OF HEY Y'ALL!

"The best way [to reach out] is to send an email and say, 'Hey, I'd love to work with you if you have anything you think I would be right for.' Add your website and/or send a PDF, and that's great. You can also go to portfolio reviews or other photo events. You can DM people on social media…really any way you can think of to get in touch with people. However, do *not* call people on personal phones or show up at home addresses!"

— AMY FEITELBERG, FREELANCE PHOTO DIRECTOR AND PRODUCER

"I suggest reaching out via email whenever possible. If you can't locate a creative's email, look them up on LinkedIn. Before reaching out there, see if they have contact information in their profile. If not, send a brief message kindly asking them if they would be open to sharing their email so you can reach out to share work more formally. In that first interaction, include a call to action. Ask for the meeting! Alternatively, ask how they prefer to be kept up to date with new work. Ask if there is something particular they are looking for. Giving a creative or a producer a reason to reply will start a dialogue and help them remember you as you continue to reach out."

— JENNIFER PERLMUTTER, SENIOR PHOTO AND MOTION REPRESENTATIVE

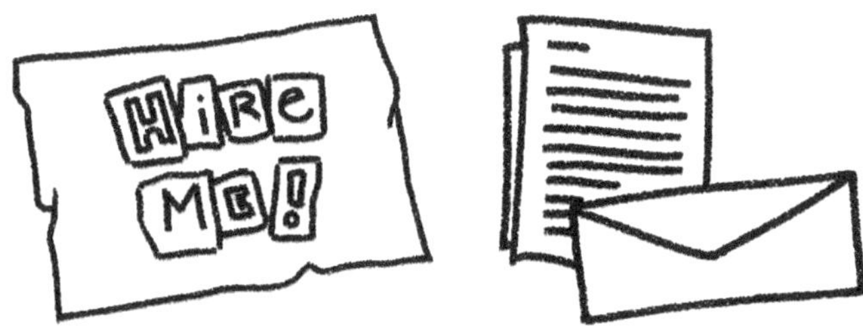

THE DOS & DON'TS OF ASKING FOR INTRODUCTIONS

In this industry, a warm introduction can feel like winning the lottery. When someone connects you with a key person in their network, they're giving you their stamp of approval and putting their reputation on the line for you. It's not something you should take lightly or ask for frivolously. If you perform poorly, not only could it harm your own reputation—you could end up blacklisted. It could also look bad for the person who originally introduced you. Their colleagues may question their judgment going forward. Like I said, a referral is not something to take lightly. Treat every referral with the utmost respect and responsibility.

There are private social media groups exclusively for photo editors, directors, and creatives, where we swap referrals, discuss the kinds of photographers we're looking for, and share our positive (and negative) experiences of working with certain people. We write glowing recommendations for photographers we've loved working with—and give warnings about those we haven't. I don't say this to scare you but to remind you: your reputation precedes you.

If you're planning to ask for introductions within your network, follow these key guidelines to keep your reputation in the clear:

Be Respectful

Maintain professional boundaries when asking someone for an introduction. Don't message someone on their personal device unless you're already friends or have an established connection. Many photographers try to push boundaries, and occasionally, male photographers will flirt with female contacts, hoping to secure gigs—an absolute no-no. This approach doesn't encourage people to pass along your information: quite the opposite. Only ask for a warm introduction if you have a close, professional relationship. Otherwise, you need to find the information yourself.

Be Intentional

Generic emails and introductions just don't work. Remember, you need to be strategic. For example, if you're reaching out to a food magazine, don't send them wedding photography—it just doesn't make sense. Be intentional in your outreach: research the publication or brand, understand their style, and make your pitch specific. Propose a unique or creative idea, and always include a clear call to action.

Don't Be Spammy

Avoid stalking or harassing people, and don't follow up excessively asking for updates. It suggests you're going to be a nightmare to work with. The higher up the ladder you go, the less likely you are to get a response—especially with cold calls and texts. Only reach out again if you've had a warm introduction or met them previously in a portfolio review. And never text asking for work—keep professional boundaries in place. If someone gave you their number in a work capacity, respect that—it does not mean you are friends. Just don't do it! Those are *immediate* deletes.

Don't Be Demanding

Only approach someone for a referral if you have already built an established relationship with them. It's a very fine line. If I know that your work is not going to be a good fit for that brand or publication, it's just going to be a waste of time. It's like asking for a recommendation when you know you're not qualified. If I haven't worked with you before, I won't feel comfortable connecting you with my network. Remember, your reputation follows you. If you do a poor job after a referral, it reflects poorly on me. That's my reputation that takes a hit.

Don't Be a User or a "Taker"

Give more than you receive (and make sure it's of value)! Don't waste people's time. I've had photographers reach out to me after seeing I moved to a new company, pretending to congratulate me but ultimately asking for inside information or connections. That's a red flag. If you're not close, don't use flattery or insincere congratulations to get something from someone. That's just a big no-no and certainly not appreciated.

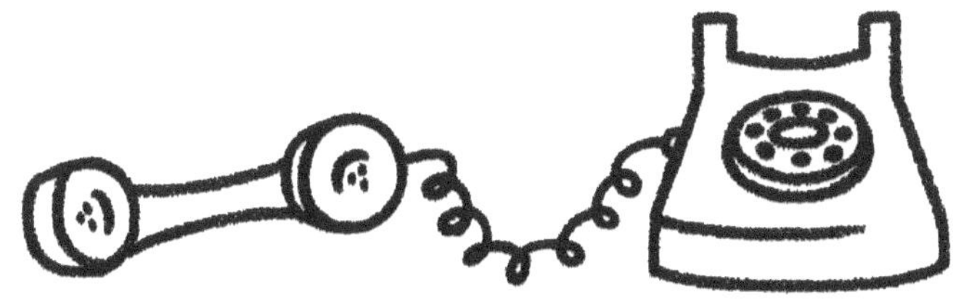

DON'T CALL US. WE'LL CALL YOU... MAYBE. BUT PROBABLY NOT.

Knowing who's in the room and understanding their role is half the battle. Once you've done your research and nailed your pitch, don't be discouraged if you don't hear back right away. Remember: just because you've sent the perfect email pitch with a twist they can't refuse doesn't mean you'll land the gig immediately. It's all part of the process. Stick to proper etiquette, and don't be afraid to follow up after a few weeks.

Now that you know who's in the room, what they do, and who you should reach out to, it's time to talk about your budget. When you do hear back from a photo editor, they'll want to discuss your rates—and you better be worth it!

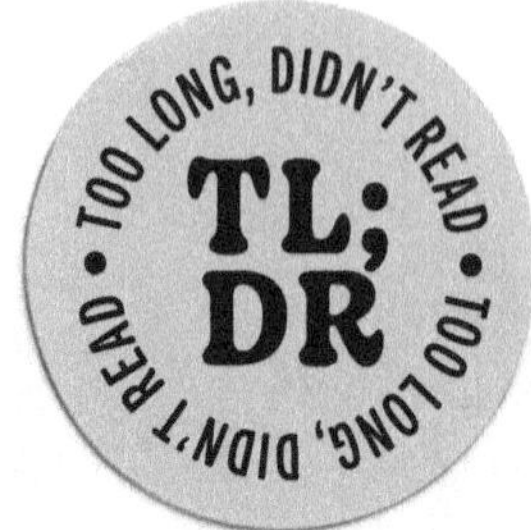

- *Always* know who is in the room and what they do.

- Do your research! It can make or break your career!

- Always be curious about someone else's perspective. It goes a long way on the job!

- If you don't know who to reach out to, start with the photo editor.

- Remember: people are busy and may not respond. Don't be afraid to follow up in a few weeks.

- If you're reaching out to someone higher up, you better have a previous connection and a standout pitch.

- Believe it or not, there are dos and don'ts to asking for introductions.

- Don't ask people to put their name on the line for you if they don't know you. That's just not cool.

- There are rules of engagement when it comes to networking. Stick to these boundaries, and everything will be fine.

CHAPTER 5

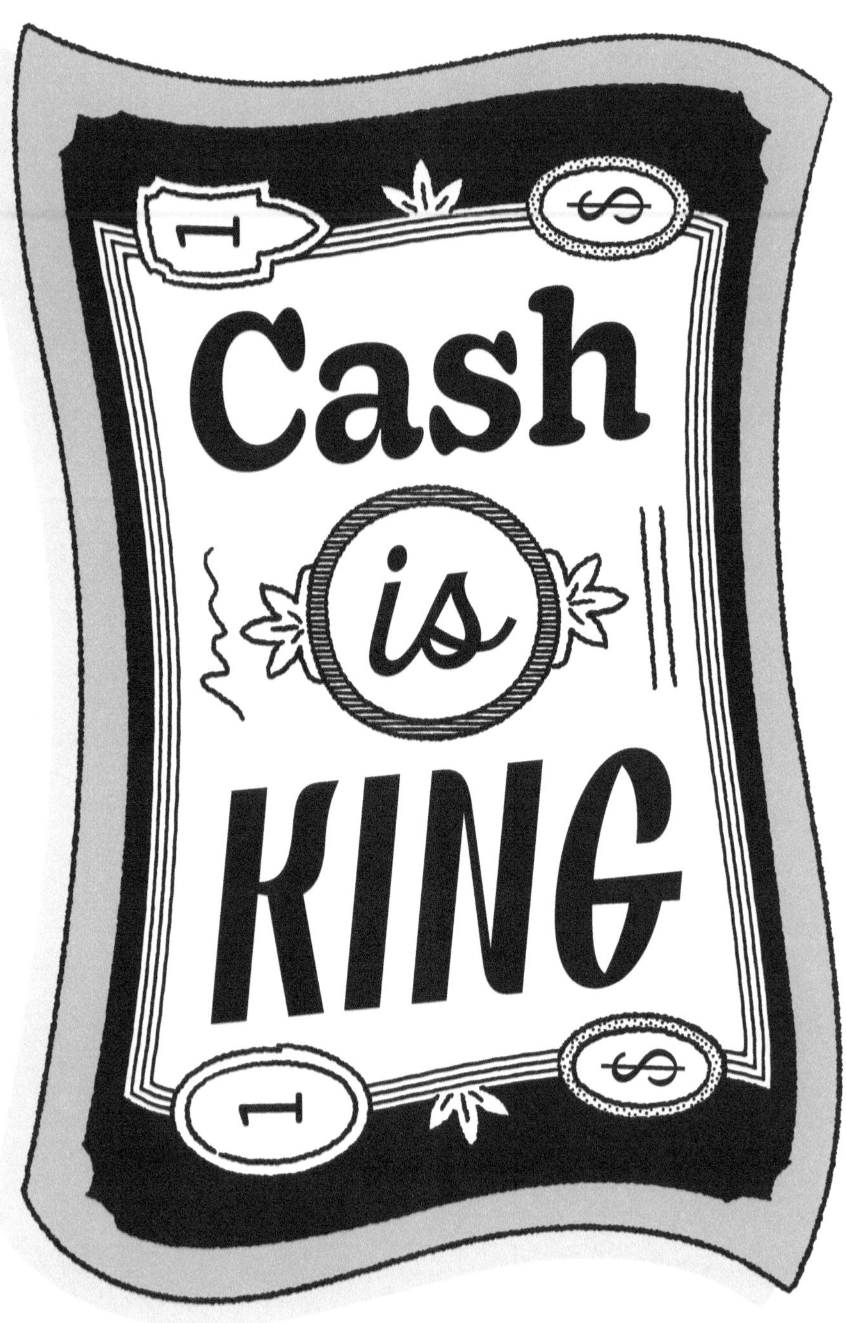

"Knowledge is power. Know your dollars and cents. Know your money. Educate yourself. Understand where you're at financially. Create a goal and know where you want to be. And that will help you know which jobs to take and which to turn down: the jobs that are worth it and the ones that aren't."

—BLACK VISUAL QUEEN

Disclaimer: Before I begin this chapter, I want to clarify that I'm not a financial professional. Any advice, quotes from my colleagues, or tips from bookkeeping or tax experts are meant as general guidance. For personalized advice tailored to your business or specific situation, please consult a local professional. They'll be best equipped to help you get started with your business, answer questions, and help you navigate the journey ahead.

What kind of coach or mentor would I be if we didn't discuss the one thing that truly makes your business a real business? That's right—in this chapter, we're diving headfirst into your business finances. Money makes the world go 'round. I know many photographers who want to shoot for big brands, thinking that's where the money is. But here's the truth: just because a brand or company is big doesn't mean they're willing to pay the big bucks—especially for photoshoots.

That's why it's so important to know the basics of your finances before you start diving into conversations about rates, estimates, and contracts. Sadly, this is where many photographers—and frankly, many people—get into trouble. Chances are, if you didn't go to business school, if you're not a professional CPA or accountant or Dave Ramsey, for that matter, you're probably learning as you go—and that's okay! But you must know where you stand financially before you can determine your rates. And if you're just hanging your hat on the idea that shooting for big brands will get you where you need to be, you're in for a rude awakening.

RATES RISE AND FALL WITH THE ECONOMY

Rates rise and fall with the economy, and companies can only spend at the rate money is flowing. When the economy is in a recession, that will be reflected in the rate you're offered for a project. I've seen it so many times, and often, the creative department's budget is the first to get cut.

I get it. It's frustrating. You put in your bid, you put in your estimates, and all you hear are crickets. Hear me on this: people aren't trying to ghost you. They're not trying to be secretive. It's most likely because of budget constraints or a non-disclosure agreement (NDA) that prevents them from being fully transparent. I want you to know this because I don't want you to be surprised when you get asked to sign an NDA before you can start talking numbers, rates, and estimates (more on that in Chapter 6). The bottom line? It all comes back to you. Understanding your finances will help you decide if taking a job makes sense—especially because of the economy.

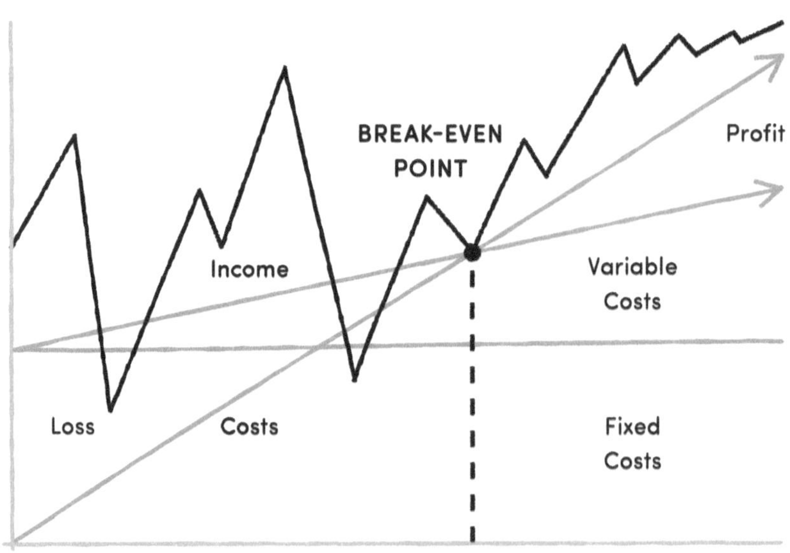

BREAK-EVEN ANALYSIS

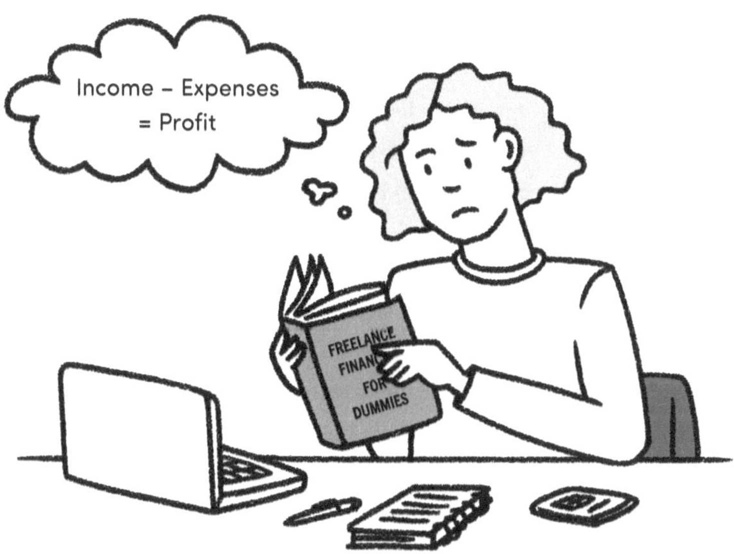

GET SMART ABOUT YOUR FINANCES

Whether you're a freelancer, part-time photographer, or shooting as a hobby, it all comes back to one thing: cash. As a freelancer, you'll have a *lot* of expenses to cover, so it's important to know how much you need to break even or make a profit. If a larger job is paying you pennies for the amount of effort required, it's probably not worth it for you (or your wallet). Similarly, with smaller jobs, knowing exactly how many you need to take on will help you meet your financial goals each month.

Keep in mind that on the editorial side, the rate is typically dictated to you. While the budgets are smaller, the trade-off is that you have more creative freedom. These lower-paying projects often offer the exposure you need to land those higher-paying, bigger-brand jobs down the road.

The question becomes, do you have the margin to take on a lower-paying editorial assignment in exchange for potential exposure? This is why you need to understand your finances as a freelance photographer. Once you know your financial situation, making these decisions will become second nature. If you're new to all this, look for free or affordable budgeting resources online or even at your local library. There are so many resources out there for new businesses—be sure to utilize them!

NEW BUSINESS BASICS

Starting a business "the right way" can feel intimidating, especially without a degree in business or finance. But you don't need a degree to succeed. All you need is a willingness to research, ask questions, and seek advice from professionals who can help you build a solid foundation.

1. Get Organized

Tanya Hirschy, owner of Tidy Books, shares:

> There are unique challenges and opportunities in running a photography business. My biggest advice is not to let the financial details get put on the back burner. I've seen too many photographers with regrets about their current financial situation because of neglect in this area. It's never too late to get organized and in control, though!

Cynthia Black, owner of Cynthia Black Books, stresses the importance of keeping things organized when you're starting your business: "Have separate bank and credit card accounts for your business and try to run all your business transactions through them. Keep personal transactions separate."

2. Protect Yourself

It's important to have the right protection in place for your business, especially in case a job goes awry. Make sure you have insurance and an employer identification number (EIN) to keep your Social Security number (SSN) safe. The more separation you can have between yourself and your business, the better. Cynthia Black advises that you don't need to be an LLC or S-Corp to operate your business—being a sole proprietor and setting up your license as a DBA (doing business as) if your business name differs from your own is perfectly fine. Do your research and consult with a business professional to choose the right structure for your business.

3. Always Have a Cushion

Owning your own business means that your income can be unpredictable. You don't have the luxury of knowing exactly when your next paycheck will come in. That means it's extremely important to keep a financial cushion for those months when business is slow. Cynthia Black recommends a reserve of two to three months' expenses:

> When you're starting out, this can be challenging because you may not be as flush with cash. But it is best to be a bit stingy and conservative with your spending for the first year or two, or when things are slow, so you can save as

much as possible and build your business. Any amount of net profit you make is taxable, so you have to factor in earmarking a percentage of those funds for taxes that you can't touch. It's a worthy investment to consult with a financial professional to figure out ways to save money, trim the fat on your spending, and maximize your deductions so you have a smaller tax burden. When your income goes up, your burn rate also goes up, so start small.

4. Seek Out the Help of a Professional

It's hard to spend money when you don't necessarily have it yet, but getting professional advice is one of the best investments you can make—for you and your business. Consider hiring someone to set up bookkeeping software (like QuickBooks or FreshBooks) or consulting a tax professional (like a CPA) to guide you on business setup, saving strategies, tax deductions, separate accounts, and estimated payments. This knowledge is invaluable and will keep you from getting slapped with a massive bill from the IRS down the road.

INSIDER TIP:

"Open at least two business savings accounts from the beginning. One is to set aside money for taxes (25 percent is recommended), and the other is to create a buffer in your business to account for low-income months. Creating this savings buffer will save you so much stress and allow you to continue operating even in low-income or high-expense months. The number one mistake I see photographers make is to pay themselves too much. This leads to having no cash flow from month to month, going into debt, and often a failed business. Determine how much your business can afford to pay you each month and be disciplined about not taking too much owner's draw."

—TANYA HIRSCHY, OWNER OF TIDY BOOKS

WHAT SHOULD I CHARGE?

As a photographer, the answer to this question really depends on your talent, consistency, and professionalism. Take a hard look at your work, your portfolio, and client feedback. If your customer feedback matches your portfolio, you're in a good position to charge higher rates for your time and artistic eye. But if your portfolio tells a different story than your customer, you've got a problem. No one wants to hire you and then be bamboozled on the other side of the job. I know because I've been there.

If you're aiming for those high-end luxury brands, you need to assess your talent level. Are you at the top of the top yet? If not, that's okay—just keep honing your craft. Top photographers charge $8,000 to $10,000 per day because they have proven themselves and their talent time after time. If you're new, you may not get those rates immediately, but don't sell yourself short.

Get right with your money. Understand your finances; go to professionals and get the education you need to make smart decisions with your money and career. Talk to other photographers and professional photo organizations to get a sense of the market and the standard rates. (Not everyone will share their exact rates with you, but it's helpful to get a range as a starting point.)

Back when I was just starting out, I made a cross-country move to San Francisco. And let me tell you, it's not cheap. I took a $10,000 pay cut, hoping it would pay off. And years later, it did. That move and all that hustle to make ends meet made a massive difference in the caliber of my portfolio—and has landed me more gigs than I can count, including rate increases as I went from job to job. And on top of all that? I loved it. It's all about taking calculated risks and knowing your worth.

INSIDER TIP:

"Day rates can go from $500/day including usage for editorial to $10,000+ per day with usage added on top for an advertising buyout. I would inquire about the full budget and try to make your fee no less than 20 percent of that."

— REBECCA KARAMEHMEDOVIC, FOUNDER AND PARTNER AT SWAY NY

INSIDER TIP:

"Rates can vary greatly and often depend on the type of client and what that particular activation can support. For example, an emerging beauty brand may not be able to support a $7,500/day rate, but that may be in scope for a larger company. I like to start high, knowing I can come down to meet a budget, and I like to be upfront by saying, 'My day rate for this usage typically starts at $4,000/day. Can your budget support that? If not, I am open to having some flexibility.' Or, if you don't know the usage, you can say, 'My rate ranges between $4,000 and $7,000/day depending on the usage. Can you share that with me?' Do not be scared to quote yourself high, as long as you accompany that with your willingness to have a conversation and be flexible, depending on the ask. Sometimes, we will take the lower rate to work with great creatives and make great work. Other times, it's important to put our foot down so we protect ourselves from not delivering on what we promise."

— JENNIFER PERLMUTTER, SENIOR PHOTO AND MOTION REPRESENTATIVE

KNOW WHEN TO SAY NO

As a photographer, remember you're a business owner first and a photographer second. Clients may not always understand your worth, so you need to get comfortable with turning down opportunities that don't pay you fairly or align with your goals.

As your portfolio evolves and your skills and business grow (and get a "glow-up"), so should your rates. The key question is: What are you willing to walk away from? If a client offers a low rate but promises future opportunities, is it worth it? Or will the project stretch your budget and cause you more stress without adding value to your portfolio? Only you can answer that.

A NOTE FROM KAREN:

Listen, I know this is a lot of information, and right now, you may be feeling overwhelmed and unsure of how to navigate contracts, estimates, rates, finances, and all of the other aspects of starting out as a professional photographer. But before you believe the lie that you don't have what it takes, let me remind you: you don't have to do it alone!

Photography can be a lonely pursuit, but it doesn't have to be. Joining a professional photographer association of some kind is crucial. These associations provide an instant, like-minded community in an industry where it often feels like you're on your own. These associations become your go-to source for questions, troubleshooting, and even a place to find and develop a network of photographer friends. So, if you're feeling unsure about building your brand, setting rates, creating estimates, contracts, copyrights, and handling business finances, these associations will become your lifeline. They can also be a lifesaver when money is tight, and you don't have the funds for an agent, accountant, or attorney.

Find a national organization that interests you and see if they have a chapter in your area. You won't regret it! Not only can you get business help and build community, but you can also enter contests, ask for peer reviews, and even get exposure through their social channels. These organizations really have your back and want to help you succeed!

Here are some of the major associations to begin your search with:

- **American Photographic Artist (APA):** Geared toward brand photographers.

- **American Society of Media Photographers (ASMP):** Another great option for brand photographers.

- **National Press Photographers Association (NPPA):** Focused on photojournalists.

- **Royal Photographic Society (RPS):** The British Institute's oldest photography association.

- **Professional Photographers of America (PPA):** Geared toward the retail side of photography, like portraits and weddings.

There are a lot of associations out there—these are just the major ones. There are also niche associations for specific photography interests. Here are a few:

- **Diversify Photo**: For photographers of color looking to flip the script of the photo industry.

- **Women Photograph**: For women and nonbinary visual journalists worldwide.

- **Focus on Women**: Aiming to elevate women in photography.

Get involved...It will be one of the best things you can do for you and your business!

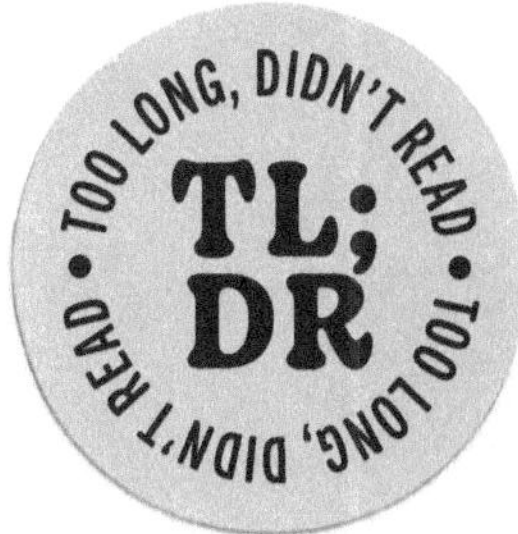

- Get smart with your money.

- Seeking help from a business professional (CPA, bookkeeper, or tax specialist) early on will set you up for success.

- Keep your business and personal finances separate.

- Know your break-even point and target profit.

- Charge what you're worth, but be open to flexibility when necessary.

- If you're charging your worth and not happy to lower your rates, you have to ask yourself if you're willing to walk away. And that's a decision that only you can make.

- Know your value and what you're willing to put up with along the way.

- Join a photography association — it will open up a wealth of resources right at your fingertips. Start with the American Photographic Artist (APA), then find one that suits your style of photography. There are so many out there to choose from!

- Cash is *still* king! The economy, rates, and budgets function at the speed of cash. In order to get a sense of a company's rates, just look around. The economy is a great indicator of how well a company is doing.

INTERMISSION 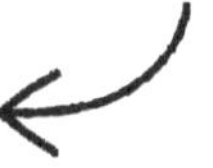

If you're enjoying my book so far, would you mind taking a moment to leave me a review on Amazon? your feedback will help me reach as many photographers as possible and break down the barriers to entering the photo industry. Remember, sharing is caring! Thank you!

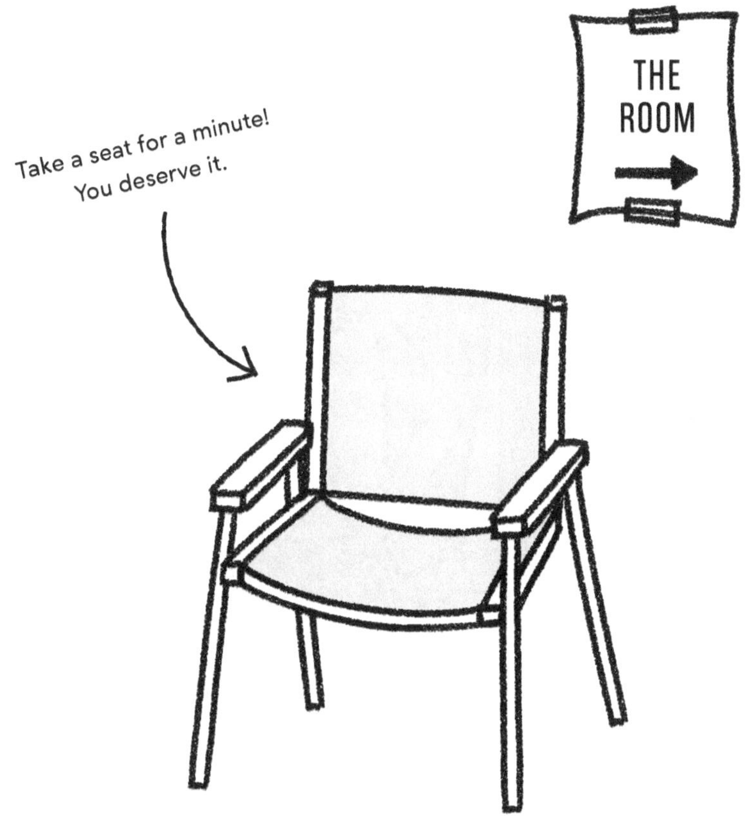

PART 2
NOW YOU'RE IN THE ROOM

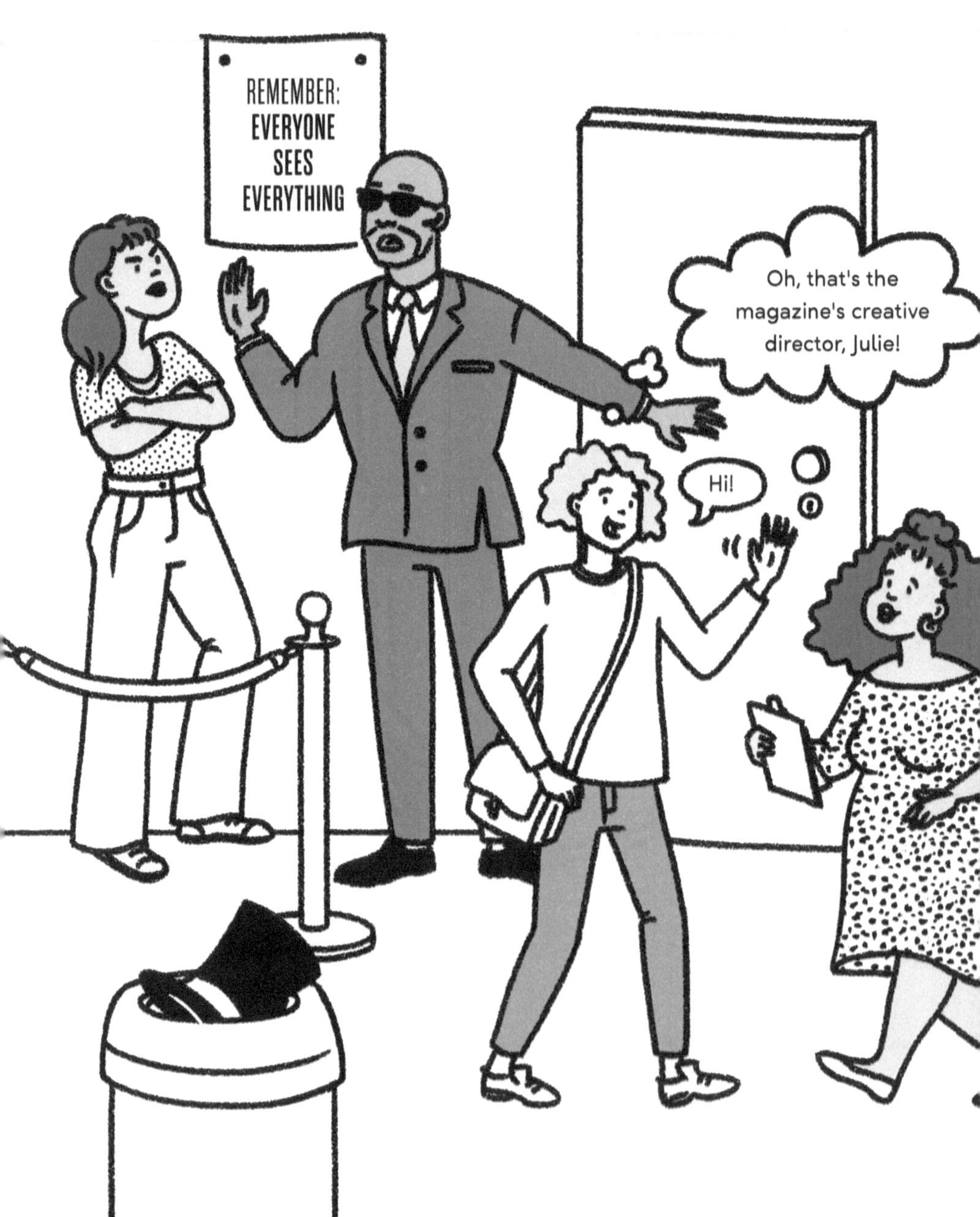

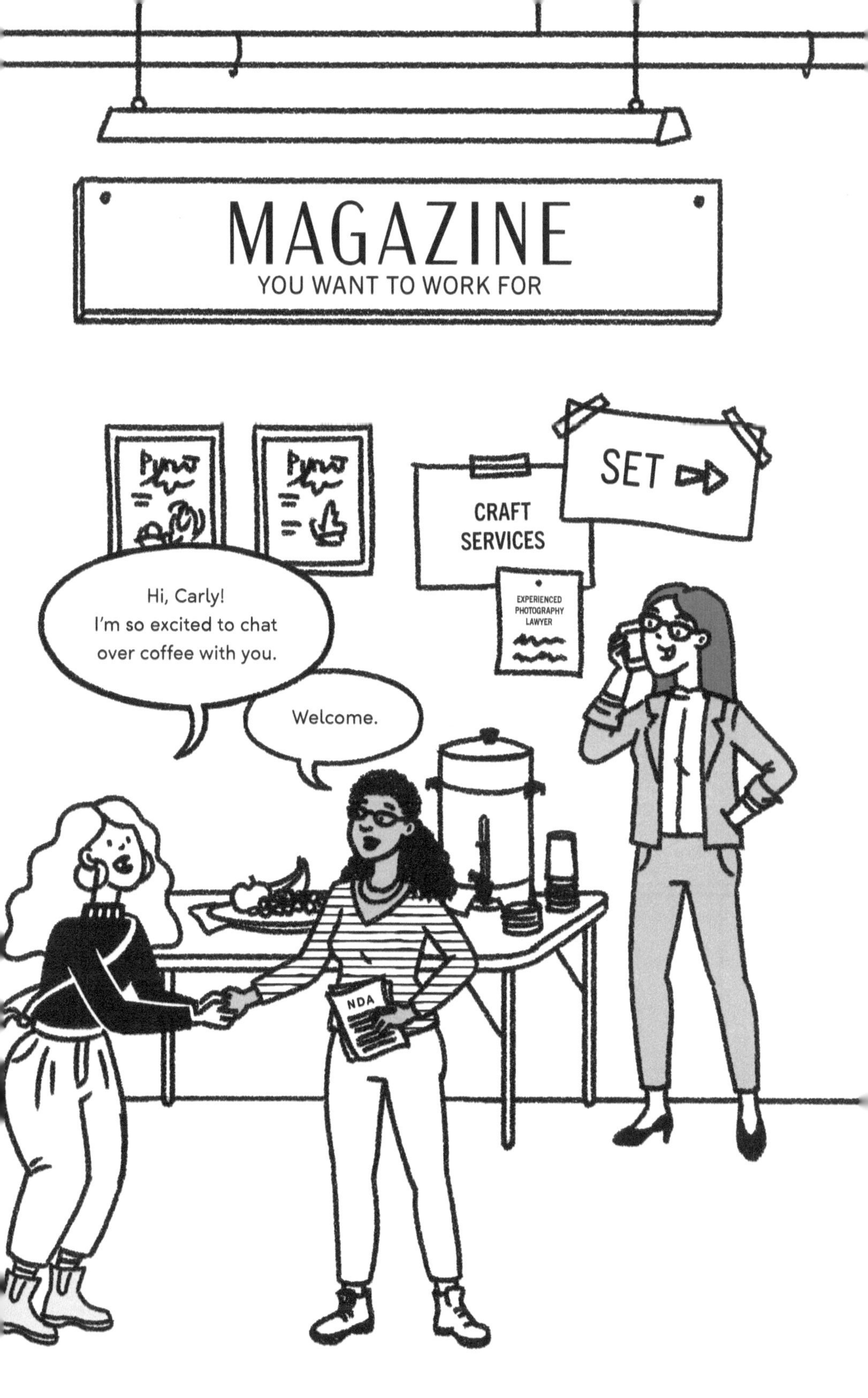

MAGAZINE
YOU WANT TO WORK FOR
PRINT
PRINT
CRAFT
SERVICES
SET
EXPERIENCED
PHOTOGRAPHY
LAWYER
Hi, Carly!
I'm so excited to chat
over coffee with you.
Welcome.
NDA

CHAPTER 6

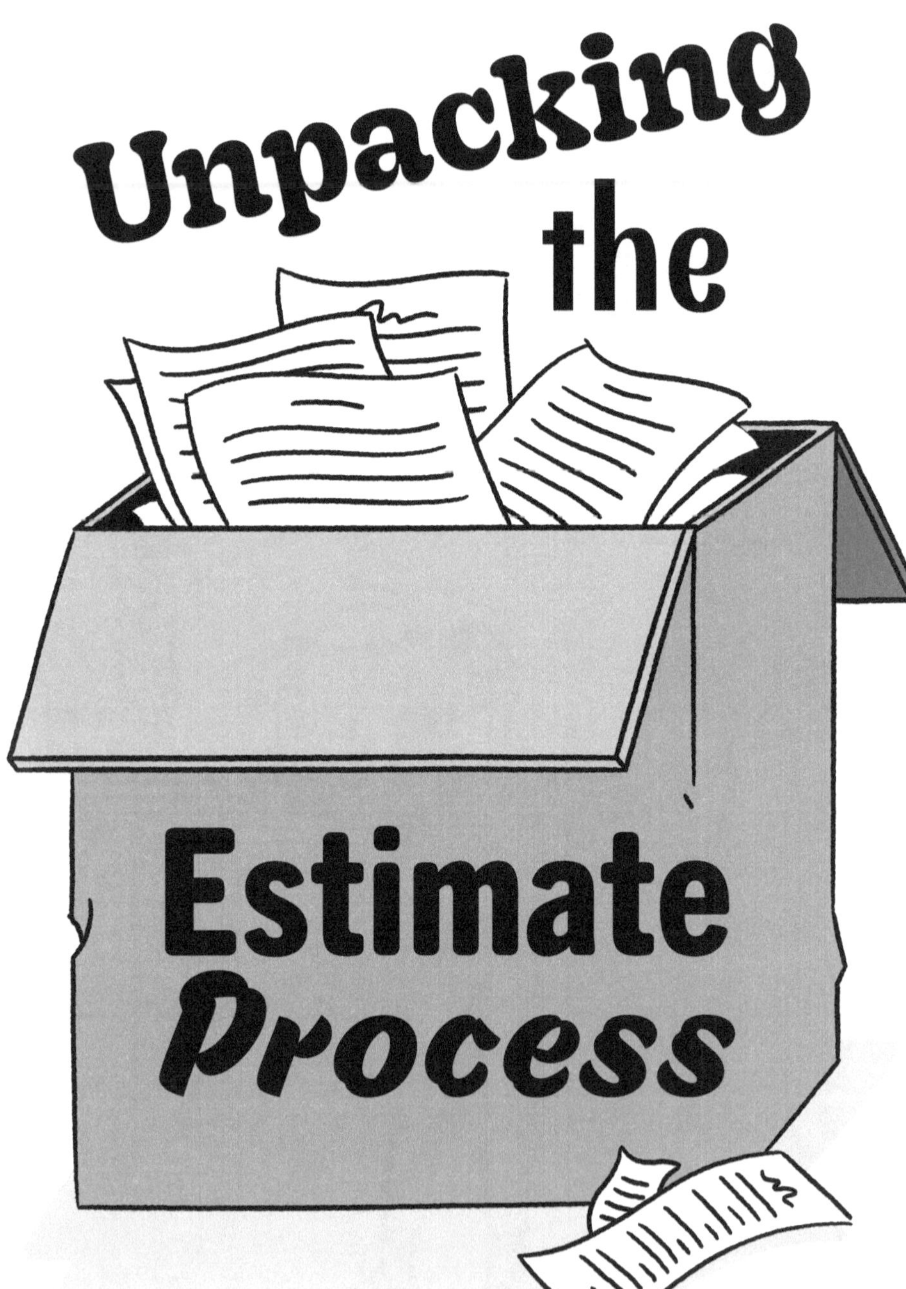

"The estimate process is going to be different for each job because each job is going to be different."

—BLACK VISUAL QUEEN

Congrats! All your hard work up until this point has paid off—you've gotten a response from that big brand you've always wanted to work with! Go ahead and do a little dance... I'll wait. Now that you've gotten a response, it's time to work through the details of the job, like rates and estimates. This is often the part that trips up most photographers—asking the company what their rate is for the shoot and not getting a clear answer.

Frustrating, right? How are you supposed to know if this job will cover your bills or pay what your time, talent, and effort are worth?

Let me give you some insight: as frustrating as it may be, most companies or big brands won't share financial details with you until you sign an NDA. They want to ensure that you won't share their financial information with the world before they provide you with the full details of the job.

DO NOT PASS GO UNTIL YOU SIGN AN NDA

According to Merriam-Webster, an NDA is "an agreement in which a person (such as an employee) agrees to keep information (such as a trade secret) confidential."[15]

If you feel like you're hitting a brick wall when asking about industry rates and estimates, *that's* why. That NDA prevents them from sharing financial details, and it's also why you're not hearing anything from other photographers either. Chances are, they've signed an NDA, too, and their lips are sealed. This is where having a good lawyer on your side becomes crucial. They'll help you navigate and understand a contract before you sign, making sure you're not getting the short end of the deal. Companies usually have their legal team protecting their interests, so you need someone to fight for you, too.

As a photo editor, I often communicate with photographers about the job details, and I'm usually the one who sends the NDA. However, it's important to note that photo editors, directors, and creatives don't create the NDA—that's the job of the brand's legal team.

So, if you're uncomfortable signing it, that's perfectly okay. But be aware that by not signing, you may be risking the job. While it's not guaranteed, I may be instructed by my team that we can't work with you for legal reasons. At that point, it's out of my hands. So, if you're getting crickets from your industry contact, that's why. If you do choose to sign the NDA, you're in the green, and you can finally pass Go. Now, it's time to move forward with the estimate process.

SEARCH

Q Should my estimate include . . .

Q Should my estimate include **my day rate?**

Q Should my estimate include **travel and lodging?**

Q Should my estimate include **fees for editing?**

Q Should my estimate **be based on the shoot time?**

ALL ABOUT ESTIMATES

Alright, I promised to keep it real with you, and that's what I'm going to do: the estimate process can be frustrating. Even after signing the NDA, companies still may not be fully transparent with you about their budget. They expect you to come up with the numbers yourself and submit them—sometimes without much guidance. For newbie photographers, especially in brand photography, this can be super intimidating. According to Merriam-Webster Dictionary online, an estimate is "a rough or approximate calculation" or "a statement of the cost of work to be done." [16]

Some companies will give you a day rate and not much else, leaving you to fill in the blanks. But on the bright side, there may be times when the company offers you more clarity: "Here's our budget for the project, this is our standard rate for shoots, and here are some line items you need to include." That's the best-case scenario. If this happens to you, consider yourself blessed!

More often than not, though, you'll encounter a combination of both scenarios. Either way, you need to do the groundwork to determine the numbers so you can generate the most accurate estimate possible. But to get there, you need to fully understand the job details—and that means asking questions...and I mean a *lot* of questions.

QUESTIONS YOU SHOULD BE ASKING *BEFORE* SUBMITTING YOUR ESTIMATE

Before you even think about putting an estimate together, you've got to get all the information. And the only way to get that is by asking the right questions. If you've never put an estimate together before, keep these questions in your back pocket and come back to them often. You'll be glad you did. Remember, not all companies are going to be forthcoming with their financial details. Often, people in my position have to function on a need-to-know basis, and sometimes that includes the budget itself.

If we do share the budget for the shoot, understand that it's likely not the full amount earmarked for paying you. The shoot budget might be just one part of a larger production within a campaign. So, if you're meeting with someone and they're not quick to offer up any information, assume you need to start playing the game of Twenty Questions. On our side, we're often *encouraged* to keep certain details private (crazy, I know!). Come to the meeting armed with everything *you* need to ask to create the most accurate estimate possible.

- **Rates**

You may not get a straight answer to this question, but it's worth asking: Does the company or brand offer a standard day rate? If they do, find out what it is. If they don't, you may need to come up with a rate yourself and hope it aligns with their budget.

- **Location**

Start by confirming the shoot location. If it's not local to you, ask if they'll cover travel, meals, and lodging—and if so, to what extent. Clarify whether they're paying for these expenses upfront or if you'll be reimbursed later.

- **Time**

Ask how many days the shoot will last and the expected hours per day. Knowing this information will help you create the most accurate estimate possible.

- **Usage & Licensing**

Find out if the company will cover usage and licensing fees and if these terms are negotiable. How do they plan to use your photos? Is this a full buyout, or are they licensing the images for a limited time (for example, three years) with the option to renew? Their answers to these questions should drastically impact your pricing and fees.

• **Production & Post-Production**

Ask if they expect the entire unedited set of photos or if they want you to handle the editing. Will any special equipment be needed for the shoot, and if so, are they providing it, or do they need you to bring your own? Clarify if they have a DigiTech or assistant available to help during the shoot; if not, are they willing to cover these additional costs?

Keep these questions on hand, and don't hesitate to ask as many as necessary to create the best and most accurate estimate you can. Showing up to a shoot only to realize you drastically underestimated your time and value is something you want to avoid at all costs. If you're working with an agent, they can guide you through this process, as they understand the nuances and typical charges associated with a great shoot. But if you're new to this and don't have an agent, you'll need to come prepared with these questions. In a perfect world, the client would provide full transparency on rates, what they will cover, and the budget—but as you and I both know, this isn't a perfect world. No one wants to show their cards, and everyone wants to put their side of the deal first.

INSIDER TIP:

"The most important thing to understand before putting a brief together is what a successful project looks like to the client. You should really understand all components of the shoot, including: Is there a photo brief, swipe, or shot list? How many shots are to be captured? Is it static/photo only, or is motion needed? What are the location details? What are the talent needs? How many clients will attend? Who will oversee the shoot? What sort of crew do they have in mind? What are the licensing/usage terms expected?"

— CHRISTINA COOKSEY, FOUNDER OF CEILING TRAIN

WHAT GOES INTO AN ESTIMATE?

When creating your first estimate for a shoot, it's good practice to create a few different kinds. Here are three versions to use as guidance:

1. The Bells and Whistles Estimate: This is your dream budget, where you factor in anything and everything you'd want for a perfect shoot. Make sure to include all potential crew members, equipment, and any special services you can think of. Then, outline the costs for each to get a full picture.

2. The Bare-Bones Estimate: This is your lean version. Think about what you can cut while still delivering quality work and making a profit. This estimate covers the essentials only.

3. The Middle-Ground Estimate: This is your middle-of-the-road estimate. This combines elements of both the all-in and the bare-bones versions. Here, you need to include your must-haves along with a few extras. This version should still ensure profitability while staying reasonable for the client.

Creating these three estimates will give you a better idea of your flexibility during the negotiation process. If the client's budget comes in lower than expected, you'll know where you can scale down while still making a profit.

Remember, no matter which estimate you go with, always allow some wiggle room. Unexpected costs can (and almost always do) arise on shoot day. Rarely does a shoot go exactly as planned or stick strictly to budget. Smart producers, editors, and directors will always hold a little money back for last-minute contingencies—and you should do the same! This cushion helps cover any unforeseen expenses and keeps you from ending up in the red.

Here are the essentials of a solid estimate. Including these elements will set you on the right track:

1. Day Rate

What do you charge for your time? Decide on your rate for the actual shoot day. If you're unsure, ask your photographer friends for guidance, and remember to charge what you're worth!

2. Pre-Scout Fees

This covers location scouting ahead of the shoot and is typically about half of your day rate.

3. Creative Fee

This is your artist fee, which may sometimes be combined with your day rate. Be prepared, however, for the company to request these as separate items.

4. Licensing Fee

Also called a usage fee, this is what you charge the client for rights to use your photos. Some photographers combine this fee with the day rate and creative fee, but often, companies will ask to see them as separate line items. Before setting this fee, you'll need to clarify how the client plans to use your images. Do they want a full buyout (where they own the images completely), or are they after a limited usage period? (Licensing and usage are covered in detail in Chapter 7.)

5. Crew

Depending on the shoot, you may need a crew. List any crew you need, such as assistants or a DigiTech, and ensure your estimate covers their pay.

6. Equipment

Detail the equipment you'll be using and note any purchases needed for the shoot. Check if the company provides any equipment, and specify what you're expected to provide. These are all essential details you need to include in your estimate to make sure it's accurate.

7. Food, Travel, Lodging, and Miscellaneous

For shoots involving travel, make sure to think about charging for lodging, meals, transportation, insurance, and taxes. Other miscellaneous line items will depend on the type of shoot you're doing. If it's a high-fashion shoot, you might need additional services like hair and makeup artists—if so, ensure their rates are included.

8. Post-Production Fee

If you're handling edits or touch-ups, add a fee that reflects the time, effort, and software needed to make this happen.

These basic line items form the foundation of your estimate. Keep in mind, though, that the estimate process will vary from job to job, as each photoshoot comes with its own unique set of requirements and line items. Just make sure you review and tailor your estimates for each new assignment, adjusting for the specific scope and needs of the project.

EXAMPLE ESTIMATE

Estimate

JOB NAME: Brand X

JOB DESCRIPTION: Environmental Portraits for Brand X's Fall Campaign. Working with talent for a 1-day shoot (up to 10 hours).

DELIVERABLES: Use of up to 15 images in perpetuity.

Client will provide location(s), location coordination, all location styling and cleaning, all employee/staff talent and talent coordination, all wardrobe/hair/makeup styling, crew meals, craft services, and all necessary COVID safety protocols.

Fees:

Creative/Licensing Fees @ $15,000.00	$15,000.00
1 Photographer Tech Scout Day(s) @ $750.00 each	$750.00

Fees Total $15,750.00

Crew:

2 First Assistant Day(s) @ $600.00 each (1 Scout, 2 Shoot)	$1,200.00
2 First Assistant Overtime Hour(s) @ $90.00 each	$180.00
1 Digital Tech Day(s) @ $750.00 each	$750.00
1 Digital Tech Overtime Hour(s) @ $112.50 each	$112.50

Crew Total $2,242.50

Equipment:

Cameras, Lighting, Grip Rentals @ $3,500.00	$3,500.00
1 Digital Tech Workstation Rental Day(s) @ $650.00 each	$650.00
Hard Drives & Media @ $250.00	$250.00

Equipment Total $4,400.00

Miscellaneous:

Insurance @ $500.00 .... $500.00

Taxes, Additional Meals, Misc. @ $500.00 .... $500.00

Misc. Total $1,000.00

Post-Production:

Retouching for up to 15 Selects and Delivery Via FTP @ $2,000.00

Post-Production Total $2,000.00

Fees Total: $15,750.00

Expenses Total: $9,642.50

Sub Total: $25,392.50

Total (USD): $25,392.50

Total (USD): $25,392.50

Now that you understand the fundamentals of an estimate, let's look at this example. This is for all my visual learners out there! Above is a middle-of-the-road, standard estimate. Naturally, your estimate may look different, with varying rates, fees, and line items depending on the client and project. If you've never seen or created an estimate before, this is a great starting point.

TRIPLE BIDS

Let's talk about triple bids. When you're asked to submit an estimate, nine times out of ten, it's likely that a few other photographers have been asked to submit theirs, too. I know that might make your heart sink a little, but what is business without a little healthy competition?

Triple bidding is a common practice for most professional organizations and companies. Brands use it to create fairness and make sure all of their options are laid out on the table. Ultimately, it all comes down to due diligence and selecting the best fit for the project.

INSIDER TIP:

"Ad agencies often reach out to three photographers or production companies to bid for the same job. These estimates usually go through a cost consultant to make sure all rates are fair and competitive. Knowing if there is a target budget number and then coming in under it is always helpful. Your estimate and treatment should be as detailed as possible with regard to what is included in each cost. Sometimes, triple bids are won based on the creativity you can provide as a photographer, but sometimes it comes down to the numbers."

— REBECCA KARAMEHMEDOVIC, FOUNDER AND PARTNER AT SWAY NY

WHAT DO YOU MEAN I'M NOT THE ONLY PHOTOGRAPHER SUBMITTING AN ESTIMATE?

If your water heater was broken, you probably wouldn't just hire the first company you find to fix it, right? Instead, you'd likely get quotes from a few different companies and compare them based on service, price, and what you can afford. The same is true for brands. They want a talented photographer who fits their project at a price that doesn't bust the budget. Now, while I can't speak for every brand, most aren't just looking for the cheapest option. We know that you get what you pay for. The sad truth is that many people understand the importance of photography, but not its true value. So, if you put in your best, most accurate bid for the job and you don't get chosen, don't sweat it. There *will* be other jobs!

I'm sharing this so you know exactly what you're stepping into when you begin the estimate process. If you're up against two other talented photographers for the same gig, it's probably wise to avoid submitting an "ask-for-everything" estimate right off the bat. Why? Because you want your bid to have a competitive edge. Does that mean you should lowball everything? Absolutely not. That only makes us question if you can deliver high-quality work. No one wants to go back and fix the photos you took—that's just a waste of everyone's time and money.

From my experience, if we want to work with you, we'll find a way to make it work. And if your estimate is above and beyond what we can afford, we'll try to negotiate. I often go back to photographers I'm eager to work with and say, "Hey, we'd love to work with you, but your estimate doesn't work with our budget. Here's our budget... Can you make this project work within that?" Submitting the best estimate for each project ultimately comes down to knowing your worth, setting accurate rates, and ensuring a fair profit margin.

WHAT HAPPENS IF THERE'S PUSHBACK?

There might come a time in the estimate process when you receive pushback on the bid you've submitted. So, what do you do? I've said it before, and I'll say it again: it all comes down to your values. If a company wants to work with you but can't swing your rates, they may ask if you can come down. Using the estimate example above, let's say you submit your bid to Brand X and they respond saying they would love to work with you…but your rates exceed their budget. They might ask if you'd consider reducing your crew size by half or cutting your rate by 25 percent. This is where the negotiations begin.

INSIDER TIPS:

"Know your floor for the project and know where you are willing to budge. For some projects, it might make sense for you to come down based on estimate requests, and for others, you might need to stick to the price. Be fair to yourself first and foremost."

— CHRISTINA COOKSEY, FOUNDER OF CEILING TRAIN

"Never be afraid to ask questions. When I submit an estimate, I always let the client know I am open to questions, thoughts, and concerns. I also let them know I am available to walk through the estimate with them if they would like. One way you could phrase this is, 'I have attached my initial estimate for your review. Please see this as a jumping-off point for conversation. If you have any questions or thoughts, I would be happy to jump on a call to chat through it.' Or, 'My estimate is attached for your review. I want to ensure I am competitive with the other bidders, so please let me know if you have any questions or concerns. I would be happy to chat through and discuss any changes that may be needed.'"

— JENNIFER PERLMUTTER, SENIOR PHOTO AND MOTION REPRESENTATIVE

HOW TO NEGOTIATE

The best negotiations happen when both parties come to the table with open minds. Avoid starting off on the defensive. When you're negotiating with a company, don't assume they're just trying to lowball you. One way to gauge their intentions is by considering the current market landscape. (Is the money flowing?) Remember, the state of the economy directly affects how much budget creative teams have for projects, and hiring a great photographer is only one part of that.

Remember when I asked you to create a bare-bones estimate that still ensures you make a profit? If you didn't initially submit it, now is the time to consider it. What could you trim from your estimate to make this project feasible? For example, if you initially included two assistants in the bid, could you get the job done with one? If you had elevated your creative fees for specific reasons, could those be adjusted at all?

This isn't about caving. That's the last thing you should do. But for negotiations to happen, each party has to give a little. Ultimately, it's up to you to determine how much you're willing to give (or cut) from your original estimate.

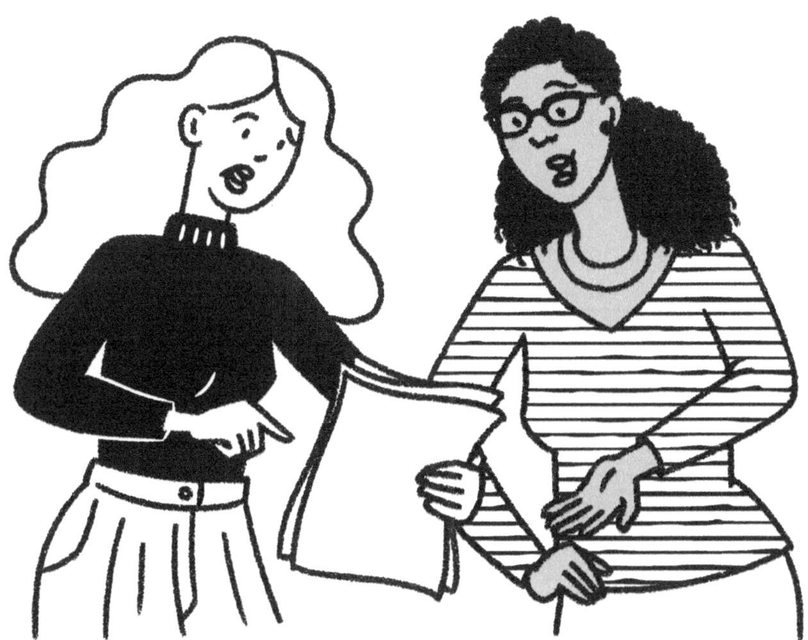

Know your nonnegotiables, too. If you consistently charge $20,000 as a creative fee and don't want to reduce it, that becomes a nonnegotiable. The same is true for your crew and equipment. If an assistant and a DigiTech are critical to getting the job done, well, then keep them on your nonnegotiable list. It's up to the company to decide whether they're willing to pay you for that. If not, you're essentially saying you're willing to risk saying goodbye to that job.

Now, after some back-and-forth negotiating, you've won the bid, and the job is yours—congratulations! But before you can dive into the project, you have to review and sign the contract. If you're not a legal expert, all the fine print might be overwhelming. Don't you dare sign that contract until you've consulted a professional to help you understand what it is, what they want from you, and what they're going to do with your images once the job is complete. In the next chapter, we're going to be talking about contracts, usage, and licensing—everything you need to know before signing your name on the dotted line.

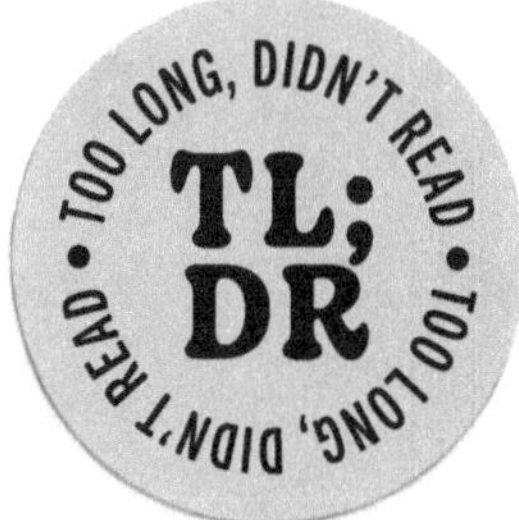

- Most companies won't discuss job details until you sign a non-disclosure agreement (NDA).

- Even after you sign an NDA, many companies still aren't very forthcoming with rates, and they're definitely not going to share their budgets. It's on you to do some digging and get the scoop!

- To submit the most accurate estimate for the job, you've got to ask questions…lots of questions. You need to find out everything you can about the job you're doing so you can create the best possible estimate for the job.

- Triple bids are a normal practice in this industry. If you think you're the only photographer up for the job, think again!

- Get in the practice of creating three estimates for each job: one that has all the bells and whistles, another that is just bare-bones (with a profit), and one that sits right in the middle.

- It's not the end of the world if a brand has pushback on your estimate.

- Negotiating doesn't mean you do the job for pennies. Know your worth and be prepared to walk away when you need to.

CHAPTER 7

Does This Look NORMAL to You?

Contracts & Licensing

Everything you make will now belong to us in perpetuity. You'll be lucky if you get payment. Offer to trade your soul for the work. No fee to kill. You are now a slave to us. You may have nothing to worry about.

IGNORE THIS

NO BIG DEAL

X ______________________________

(JUST SIGN HERE)

> *"You don't have to take the first rate*
> *or the first contract at face value.*
> *You can always, always negotiate."*
>
> —BLACK VISUAL QUEEN

Disclaimer: As I've said before, I'm not a legal professional, and every situation is completely unique. This book is not intended to provide legal advice or counsel specific to your circumstances. Please contact a qualified attorney in your area for personalized guidance on matters such as legal contracts, licensing, copyright, and more.

Contracts are often the bane of our existence—on both sides of the industry. I can confidently say that unless you're part of the legal world, chances are you don't like contracts, either. However, they remain an important part of the process, ensuring clarity, protection, and fairness for everyone involved.

In one of my previous roles, I worked as a contractor for a well-known brand. As a producer on the project, I was responsible for facilitating contracts for the photographers we hired. These contracts included a clause stating that the photographer couldn't showcase any of the work they produced for the shoot on their website, social media platforms, or anywhere else. Basically, the photographer was allowed to shoot the images, get paid, and move on. While they could display the company's logo on their site, they couldn't show the actual work they had created.

I was working with a photographer on a shoot, and a couple of days after the work went live, they posted one of the images to their social media account. Normally, this might not seem like a big deal—especially since they had posted on a story that disappears within twenty-four hours. However, it was a direct violation of the terms of the contract they had signed with the company. Ouch, right? It gets worse: one of the drastic errors this person made was that they tagged the brand in their social media story. The hard part? I had to be the "bad guy" and inform them that they had breached their contract.

This kind of thing isn't an isolated incident—it happens more often than you think. Why? Because people aren't thoroughly reading their contracts before signing them.

It is so important to know exactly what you're signing before you ever put pen to paper. That means reading every single word of every single line in the contract and fully understanding what you're agreeing to if and when you take the job. If the legal jargon feels confusing and overwhelming, that's okay—you're not alone! Many people struggle with it. That's where a legal professional can help. I know what you're thinking...cue the internal groan. I get it—that means spending more money that you might not have. But trust me, it's far better to invest in legal advice upfront than to risk breaking a contract and facing an expensive dispute in court later.

In this chapter, my goal is to empower you with the knowledge you need to confidently understand what you're signing and agreeing to when a contract hits your inbox. I want you to know what you're accepting, what should be negotiated, and the basic terms commonly found in photography contracts. Before we dive in, here's the bottom line: you don't have to take the first rate or the first contract at face value. You can always, *always* negotiate.

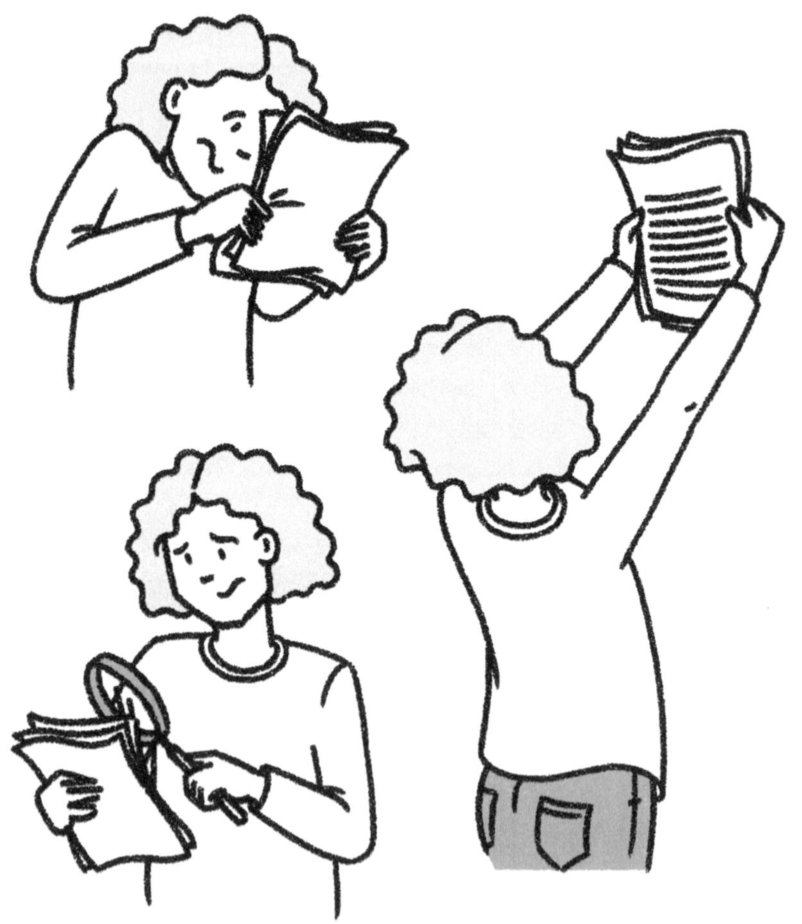

WHAT IS A CONTRACT?

A contract is an agreement between two parties, one providing a service and the other receiving it. Ninety-nine percent of the time, the contract is written to favor the service provider. So, if you're on the receiving end of a contract, do not be fooled—that contract is not designed with your best interests in mind. That's why it's crucial to take responsibility for understanding exactly what the contract states before you sign it.

If you're a professional photographer shooting for families, weddings, and other client-focused events, you know what I'm talking about. You draw up your contracts to protect yourself, your brand, and your business. When you send out your contract to your clients, you're likely not pointing out certain sections to make sure they understand or agree with the details. Instead, you just automatically expect them to read through it, ask questions if needed, and sign it.

The same principle applies to my side of brand photography. When contracts are issued, we're not encouraged to point out specific clauses or explain them. People in my position are just the middleperson—we're not out to wring you dry. These contracts and the terms within them are often above our pay grade. Our role is simply to get the contract signed and continue with the job at hand. Keep in mind, though, that the larger the company you're working with, the larger their legal team will be. These teams are dedicated to drafting contracts that protect the company's interests— no matter what.

So, as a new or seasoned photographer trying to get into the brand side of the industry, what can you do?

READ THE CONTRACT — THEN READ IT AGAIN.

The best way to know what you're signing (before you sign it) is to read every contract that comes your way thoroughly, word for word, line by line. I get it—contracts can be intimidating, and the temptation to just skim through and quickly sign your name on the dotted line is real. But it's not smart. I am empowering you as the photographer to educate yourself and ask questions. Remember, these contracts aren't written with your business in mind. That means you have to know what you're signing and advocate for yourself above all else.

FIND AN ATTORNEY TO HELP YOU UNDERSTAND THE CONTRACT.

As I said earlier, contracts can be intimidating! One of the best ways to make sense of what you're reading is by consulting someone who specializes in them. Find a lawyer or attorney who can guide you through all the legal jargon and help you understand what you're about to get into. And listen, if you join a professional photographer association, they often offer excellent resources, including access to legal professionals who can help educate you and provide direction in situations like these.

ASK QUESTIONS.

If you've been dreaming of this moment—landing a brand photography gig—you might assume that you're not able to ask questions. What if you lose out on the gig? What if your questions scare them off? Listen to me closely: *never* hesitate to ask questions, and *never* take anything at face value. I understand it may be your very first gig with a big company, and your nerves are completely valid. But remember, there's always room for negotiation in any business deal, and this is just that—a business deal. So, if you're hesitant to ask questions for fear of losing out on the gig, let me reassure you: you won't. Having questions or wanting to negotiate doesn't mean you'll lose the job. In fact, at this stage in your career, there's more risk in not asking questions. Your brand and your business are worth advocating for!

DON'T BE AFRAID TO NEGOTIATE.

One of the beautiful things about working with brands is that almost everything is negotiable—up to a point. And that point is when you sign the contract. So, do yourself a favor and mark up that contract! Sure, some brands may say, "This is it. There's no room for negotiation." If that's the case, you have a decision to make. Is this job worth what they're offering? But let me tell you—there's pretty much always been an exception in every contract I've come across. You don't have to accept everything as it is. Read it. Are there clauses you don't understand or don't agree with? Get clarification from the person presenting the contract or from a legal professional. Don't be afraid to speak up for yourself if something doesn't sit right with you. For example, you can say, "Hey, I don't agree with these items in the contract. Can we either reword this clause or negotiate the terms in this section?"

Usually, they'll come back with something like, "The legal team has agreed to this and this, but these things over here are a hard no." Understand what you can get and what you can't. Knowing what you're willing to accept—whether they budge or not—will help you decide to move forward with the job or walk away.

WHAT CAN BE NEGOTIATED?

Every company and every contract is different. So, when it comes to negotiations, some companies might be more willing to work with you, while others—especially larger companies—may be less willing to make exceptions. That being said, when it comes to contracts, some things are negotiable, and some are nonnegotiable. It's always going to depend on the company you're working with, but the key is being open to starting the conversation.

A few years back, I worked on a *major* cover project for a company that had some pretty crazy contract terms. My colleagues and I reached out to a photographer we wanted to work with. Knowing it was a big opportunity, the photographer was thrilled (can you blame them?!). They were so excited, in fact, that they signed the contract and sent it back to us within minutes. That told me right there that this photographer hadn't bothered to read through the contract. If they had, we probably would've had some pushback. Most photographers at least come back to me with, "I read it, and I have some mark-outs for you to look at." That's when the negotiations begin.

It's up to you, as the photographer, to read through the contract and decide what you're willing to accept or walk away from. Is the job important enough that you'll accept the contract terms because the work could elevate your career in the future? Are you comfortable signing a less-than-ideal contract, knowing the work might be worth it? At the end of the day, if a company isn't open to negotiation and insists you sign the contract as is, that's their prerogative. I just want you to understand the terms and clauses so you can make an informed decision on how to proceed. Now, let's get into the contract itself.

WHAT TO LOOK FOR IN A CONTRACT

Okay, let's say you can't afford a lawyer, and you have to make the best decision you can by reading each contract line by line. In this case, Google and a good dictionary are going to be your best friends. If this sounds like your situation right now, I want you to know what to look for in a contract and comprehend what those things mean.

Let's say you've got a company on the hook, and you've verbally agreed on a specific day rate, the project cost, and the main deliverables. However, when the contract comes through, something feels...a little off.

Here's the deal: contracts can be confusing and often have gray areas—usually in favor of the company. It's possible that the person you're working with hasn't fully communicated what you agreed on to the legal team (or whoever is writing up the contract), or they're trying to sneak a few things past you. I might sound like a broken record here, but *this* is why it's so important to read these contracts thoroughly. You need to know what you're looking at and what you're agreeing to!

When you go through a contract, here are the key things to focus on with the deliverables from the photo shoot in mind:

1. Who gets to use it?
2. How do they want to use it?
3. How long do they want to use it?
4. Where is it going to be used?
5. Who can use it, and who has the rights to it?
6. Do I get to take credit for the work?
7. What happens if the job changes?
8. What's the job scope?
9. How and when will I get paid?

WHO GETS TO USE IT?

Exclusivity

Is the brand or publication asking for the work to be *exclusive* to them forever? In this case, you're looking for the word "buyout" (more on that later). Alternatively, the contract might specify exclusivity for a set period—maybe five weeks, two years, or some other defined time frame. What this means is that during this exclusivity period, you cannot sell those images to a third party, display them anywhere else, or even include them in your portfolio.

If the contract specifies *non-exclusivity*, it's a bit more flexible. Non-exclusive rights often mean the company expects you to hold off on using or selling the images until their project—whether it's a story, campaign, or other initiative—is published or goes live. After that, you're free to use the images however you'd like to: in your portfolio, on your website, or even reselling them elsewhere.

HOW DO THEY WANT TO USE IT?

Usage

Now, you want to look at the term *usage*. How does the company want to use your images? Are they going in a printed magazine or newspaper? Is it a digital publication or campaign? Is it going on a billboard, in a book, or on social media? Essentially, you want to know where these images will be living once you deliver. If they're asking to publish in multiple places and mediums, then your rate needs to reflect the increased exposure. If you're doing the images for an entire brand campaign that will be shown in stores, on packaging, on billboards, and even in Times Square, you need to consider that in your pricing.

Usage Purpose

Now that you know how they want to use the images, you'll want to know what the purpose is. That term is *usage purpose*. For example, a company might want to use the image for a feature or cover story, but they don't own the image itself and won't directly profit from it. Alternatively, a company might want to use it for an entire campaign— as I mentioned earlier—leveraging your work to drive their revenue. I want you to think about this as "for profit" (commercial use) versus "not for profit" (editorial use). The purpose significantly impacts your pricing—if the images are for a major brand campaign spanning multiple mediums and generating profit, your day rate needs to reflect that higher value and *usage purpose*.

HOW LONG DO THEY WANT TO USE IT?

Duration of Use

This term specifies how long a company or brand intends to use your images. If you see the word "buyout" in a contract, it means they want to use it indefinitely, and the images essentially become theirs. In such cases, you should be tripling your day rate. While a buyout often allows you to retain copyright, some contracts may require you to surrender it completely. This is why it's so critical to scrutinize the duration of use in every contract. If a company wants you to give up your rights (or copyright) to the images, you'll often see the term "*work for hire.*" This means that any work you do for the company becomes their intellectual property. For example, let's say you're a staff photographer for a company. Any work you do for that company is their intellectual property since you are on their payroll. Basically, whatever you create for them, they own.

The next thing you want to look at is *renewal terms*. If a company says they want to use your images for a duration of seven years, then at the end of that time, you'll have the opportunity to renegotiate the terms of usage if they want to continue using them.

INSIDER TIP:

"Be careful to avoid giving away rights in your work inadvertently — always make sure you understand the documents you sign and register your work with the Copyright Office whenever possible!"

— STEPHEN MICHAEL DONIGER, ATTORNEY AND SHAREHOLDER AT DONIGER/BURROUGHS PC

WHERE IS IT GOING TO BE USED?

Locally or Globally

Many companies operate across multiple countries, so it's important to know the geographic scope of your image usage. For instance, a company might offer you a $5,000 day rate but want exclusive rights to the images with a total buyout for global, profit-driven use. In this scenario, that $5,000 day rate suddenly doesn't seem so substantial, considering that they're asking you for the world. You need to ask yourself: does the compensation they're offering match the scale and exclusivity of their request? Knowing where and how your images will be used can help you evaluate whether the terms are fair and if the job is worth it.

INSIDER TIP:

"A copyright exists in a photograph the moment it is captured — nothing need be 'done' to perfect those rights. The copyright can then be registered with the USCO, and a timely registration creates additional remedies in the event of infringement (i.e., the ability to recover statutory damages and attorneys' fees)."

— STEPHEN MICHAEL DONIGER, ATTORNEY AND SHAREHOLDER AT DONIGER/BURROUGHS PC

WHO CAN USE IT, AND WHO HAS THE RIGHTS TO IT?

Copyright

Copyright is the creator's inherent claim to their work. That means the moment you take a photo, write a book, or do anything creatively, you automatically own the copyright to it. However, simply having this inherent copyright doesn't always protect you from violations. If you care about something you've created or an image you've taken, you should register it with the US Copyright Office (USCO).

When you get into the legal system and you're fighting over copyright claims or violations, you're going to have a stronger case if you can show that you have registered the work and have a *legal* claim to it. Even though you have the inherent copyright just by being the creator, registering it adds an extra layer of legal protection and credibility. Taking this step ensures you have a solid foundation if you need to defend your rights. As said before, I'm not a legal professional, so reach out to someone qualified in this area, if needed.

Sublicensing Rights

Some companies may want the ability to allow a third party to use the images you've created, which requires a sublicense. Let's say you're working with a brand, and they say, "We want to sublicense this to another brand within our family of brands." Or they might say, "We can license these to anyone we want." Most photographers are going to have a problem with that. Why? Because you are shooting for the brand and licensing it to them, not to an unknown third party. If you see sublicensing in the contract, go ahead and raise your rate! You should get paid what you deserve—no matter who is using the images.

Modification Rights

Many brands ask for image RAWs (.raw files) and want the freedom to modify the images—often far beyond regular retouching. As the photographer, you might be okay with this, but I want to remind you that it's crucial that you know exactly how they intend to use the images. Are they going to Frankenstein the photo and rework it into a brand-new, unrecognizable image? (Sometimes, this means they're creating a different image by heavily altering elements, like chopping out an arm to use in a different context.) Or are they just making minor adjustments, like some light retouching? There's no definitive right or wrong answer here—it all depends on your boundaries and the terms you agree upon. However, knowing what the outcome will look like and how much control you're giving up is essential for making an informed decision.

DO I GET TO TAKE CREDIT FOR THE WORK?

Credit

In most cases, brands don't often give the photographer credit on the images themselves. However, you might be able to negotiate for credit by asking them to include "shot by [your name]" or "photographed by [your name]" wherever the image is used. That said, the more common scenario is that you'll shoot the images, and they'll allow you to showcase the work in your portfolio. This enables future clients to recognize and attribute the work to you, even if formal credit isn't given in public-facing materials.

WHAT HAPPENS IF THE JOB CHANGES?

Kill Fee or Termination Fee

If we "kill" the shoot a month out and nothing has happened, chances are you won't get paid anything. However, as the shoot date approaches, companies may compensate you with a percentage of the agreed-upon rate. For example, if the shoot is canceled within two weeks, you might receive 25 percent of your rate for the job. That percentage increases as the cancelation window narrows, with cancelations within forty-eight hours typically resulting in 100 percent of your agreed rate. In my experience, if we're having to cancel, it's likely because we need to reschedule. In this case, the date just gets moved, and the payment stays the same. As for the contract, always find out how much you'll be paid if a shoot gets pushed (rescheduled) or canceled.

WHAT IS THE SCOPE OF THE JOB?

Job Scope

If a contract doesn't state exactly what you're shooting and the specific deliverables expected of you, consider it a major red flag. This ambiguity could simply be an oversight—or worse, an intentional attempt to keep things vague so they can tack on whatever they want to the project. Either way, you don't want to sign a contract that doesn't have this information in black and white. That's why it's *so* important to read the contract line by line. As much as I hate to say it, some companies do try to sneak stuff in there, or their "plans change," and they don't always relay this information. Always make sure the job scope is explicitly stated to avoid any surprises later.

HOW AND WHEN WILL I GET PAID?

Payment Terms

The first thing to look for in this section is the agreed-upon rate, along with the payment terms. Usually, payment terms are net 30, meaning you'll get paid within thirty days of delivering the work. However, you might come across terms like net 60 or even net 90. Net 90 is *terrible*. If you see this, definitely try to negotiate better terms. This section should also specify what happens if the company is late with payment or if you are late delivering the work. Make sure all conditions are clearly stated to avoid any confusion or future complications.

WHAT HAPPENS IF A COMPANY VIOLATES THE CONTRACT?

Unfortunately, contract violations can happen on either side, and as a photographer, it's crucial to advocate for yourself. The contract exists to help you do just that. Let's say a company violates the usage in your contract by selling your images to a third party. The best thing you can do is go straight to a legal professional who can help you determine if pursuing the issue is worthwhile. As the photographer, the decision ultimately lies with you: do you ignore the violation or pursue litigation? It's worth noting that many companies (especially the larger ones) have big law firms behind them, who can drag out cases for what seems like an eternity—making it both stressful and expensive. The question is: do you really want to go to battle with them?

Stephen Doniger, attorney and shareholder at Doniger/Burroughs PC, explains that many copyright cases are resolved through "pre-litigation negotiations." He adds that federal courts hold exclusive jurisdiction over copyright claims, though the parties can agree to address those claims through arbitration agreements or, for smaller claims, the Copyright Claims Board (CCB). Consulting an attorney will clarify your options and help you determine the best course of action.

WHAT HAPPENS IF I VIOLATE THE CONTRACT?

Depending on the nature of the violation, this could get nasty. If the violation is egregious enough, the company may decide to come after you. In my own experience, minor infractions—like when a photographer posted the brand's image on their social media story without permission—can often be resolved easily. In that instance, I simply approached her and asked her to take it down. I chose not to escalate the situation further because I recognized the action wasn't malicious; it was just a quick, simple mistake.

However, I have also seen cases where legal has to get involved, such as when a photographer (who didn't own the copyright to the work) posted the images *everywhere*. The company's response will depend on the severity of the violation. If you find yourself in this situation, consulting a lawyer should be your immediate next step. They can help advise you on how to either de-escalate the situation and make it right or fight it in court.

After learning about contracts, I hope you're still able to keep your eyes open. Like I said, contracts are the bane of everyone's existence. But hopefully, you're catching on to the pattern here: seeking counsel from a legal professional is the best course of action whether you're reviewing a contract, fighting a violation, or just wanting to make sure everything checks out. And if it does, that's great! That means you can finally get "in the room" and start shooting for that brand or company you've been dreaming about.

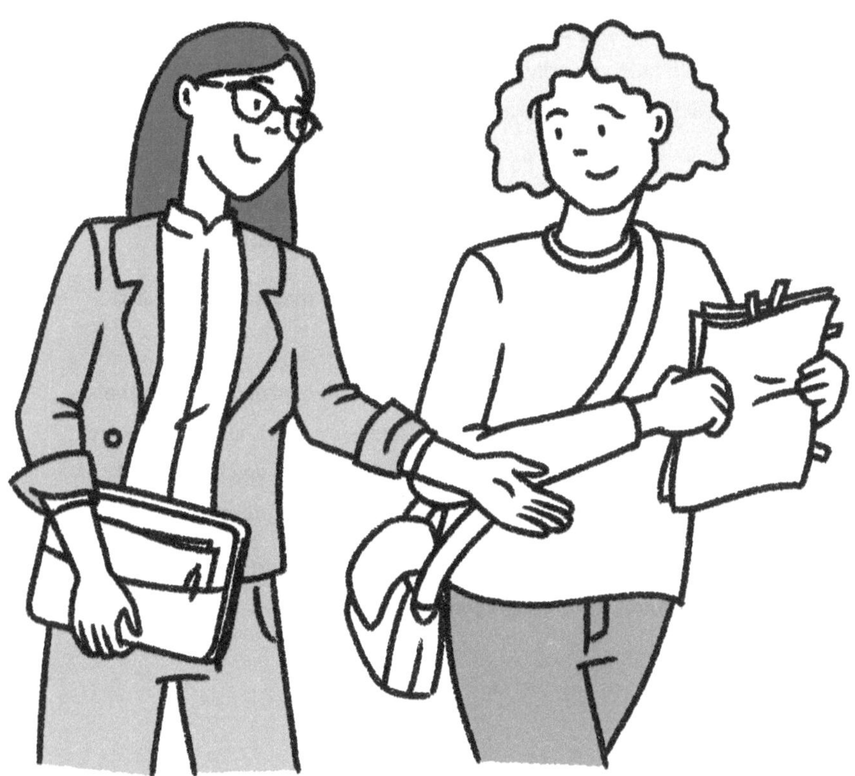

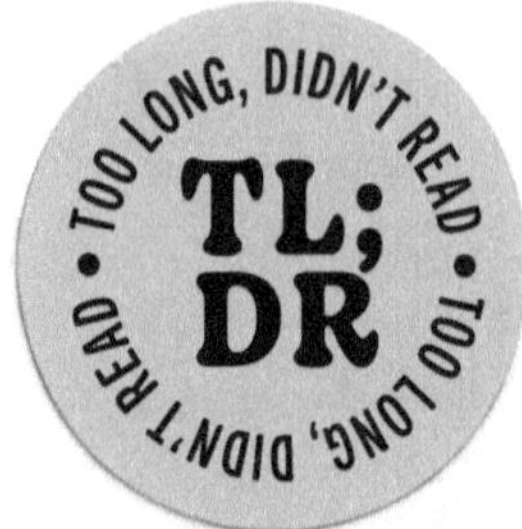

- Contracts can be so confusing. If you're not well-versed in legal jargon, it's in your best interest to find a great lawyer and ask them to review your contracts — before you sign on the dotted line.

- Never, ever, *ever* sign anything before reading it. That's just not smart.

- If you don't have the money upfront to find a lawyer, reach out to a photography association and see if they offer any resources that can help you educate yourself on contracts. Don't be afraid to reach out to your own network for help, too!

- Do not … I repeat … do not take any contract at face value. I know you want that job. I know you're excited. You're not going to risk losing the job just because you ask questions.

- Don't be afraid to negotiate! The company may say no, but it's always worth a shot.

- You get to give the final word on whether a contract is worth the work. Do your due diligence and make sure you know what you're getting into before you start the job. Make sure you know what you can and can't do with the images after the job is done.

- Contract violations happen. It's important to find the right legal help to guide you through your next steps.

CHAPTER 8

Getting the SHOT:

All Things Photo Production

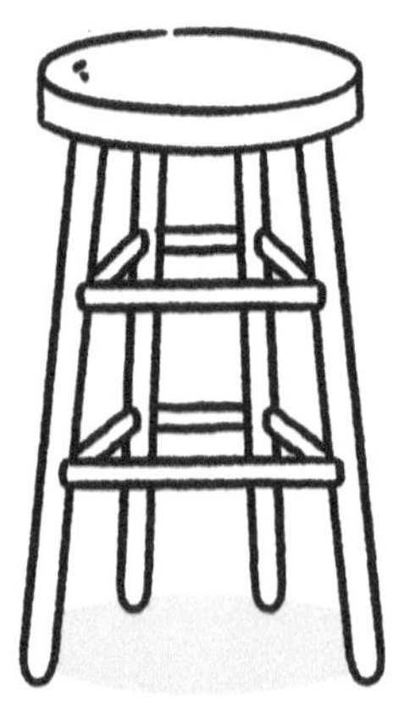
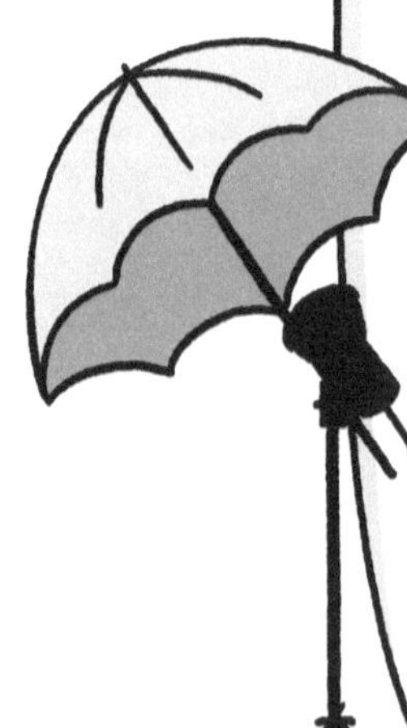

"Hope for the best and prepare for the worst—make that your mantra, and you can get through any photoshoot that comes your way."

—BLACK VISUAL QUEEN

Take a deep breath! You've made it past all the boring stuff: estimates, negotiations, and signing contracts. Now, it's off to the races for the actual photoshoot. If you're feeling intimidated and nervous right now, you're in good company. That is called imposter syndrome. Maybe you felt like you were on top of the world once you signed the contract and now, you're not even sure you know how to use your camera. I get it: that's intimidating! But don't let those first-time nerves keep you from doing what you were made to do!

I remember the first time I walked onto a professional photo set as a young photographer. I was so nervous I could barely breathe. Surrounded by expensive gear, a huge crew, and high-profile clients—it was all so overwhelming. I kept thinking, "What am I even doing here? I'm not good enough for this. They're going to find out I'm a fraud." But you know what? I showed up anyway. I pushed through the fear and self-doubt and did the work. I absorbed everything I could, watching the more experienced photographers like a hawk. I asked questions, even when I felt stupid. And, of course, I made mistakes—but I learned from them. Slowly but surely, I began to gain confidence in my skills and my place on set. Fast forward to today, and I'm now the one directing those big shoots and even leading teams of my own. To be honest, I still get nervous sometimes—that never fully goes away—but I've learned that the key to success in this industry isn't about being perfect or knowing everything. It's about showing up, doing the work, and pushing yourself out of your comfort zone. So, if you're feeling the way I did on that first set, know that you're not alone. It's okay to feel intimidated. It's okay to battle imposter syndrome. Everyone starts somewhere—embrace the discomfort, give it your all, and trust that you'll find your way as you put one foot in front of the other, one step at a time.

• • •

There are three typical phases of a standard photoshoot: pre-production, production, and post-production.

In this chapter, I'll break down each phase, explain what they entail, and share tips on how to prepare. By understanding these steps, you'll walk into your next shoot feeling confident and ready to tackle every stage like a pro.

PRE-PRODUCTION

Pre-production encompasses everything that happens *before* the photoshoot. The bigger the photoshoot, the more work (or pre-work) you need to do beforehand. You've probably heard the saying, "Hope for the best and plan for the worst." Make that your pre-production mantra from now on because, as much as I hate to tell you this, the worst often happens on the big day. Show up overprepared to give both the subject and the client confidence that you're a professional who has their stuff together. It never hurts to show up confident, knowing you've done everything needed to do your job well.

HOW TO PREPARE FOR A PHOTOSHOOT

On my side of the industry, it does *not* look good for a photographer to show up on the day of the shoot trying to figure things out for the very first time. So, what does preparing for a photoshoot entail? Every photoshoot is unique, depending on the size and scale of the shoot, who your client is, the location, and who you're shooting. But no matter how different each shoot might be, these foundational pre-work steps can help you prepare well and set you up for success *every single time*:

- **Do your location scouting in advance.**
- **Communicate early—and often.**
- **Make sure you have the right equipment...with backups.**

The pre-work phase is your time to work out the kinks in advance. It's your opportunity to think through every scenario that could go wrong and come up with solutions. By following the three foundational steps listed above, you're going to be far better off, look more professional, and be ready to handle whatever the photoshoot throws at you. Let's start with location scouting.

SCOUT OUT THE SHOOT LOCATION *EARLY*

Location scouting is so important for every photoshoot, big or small. Depending on the size and scale of the shoot, you'll either have a set number of hours or a couple of days to scout out the location beforehand. If it's a local shoot, you may be able to show up a few hours early to scout the best spots. But if you must travel to get there, it's best if you arrive a day or two early and spend as much time as you can getting to know the location and coming up with your game plan. This allows you to see the shoot location in person and plan out where to get the best shots, predict the best lighting conditions (if it's outside), and create contingency plans in case the weather goes south. This is your opportunity to prepare for almost every single scenario that could happen—good or bad.

COMMUNICATE EARLY AND OFTEN

As the photographer, one of the most important (and helpful) steps you can take to ensure a smooth shoot is to communicate early and often with your point of contact— usually the photo director or editor. For smaller editorial shoots, you might also be in charge of communicating the date, location, and time with the talent or subject directly. For example, the photo editor may initially reach out to the subject to verify what works best for them, often cc'ing you on the email. Once you've been introduced to the subject, the photo editor might release you to handle the rest, ensuring you align with the subject on key details like what they should wear and where they need to show up.

In this scenario, you're always keeping the photo editor in the know because you're running the show—especially for these one-and-done, smaller shoots. Other times, the photo editor will give you all the information and ask if you can set it up and get it done. But most of the time, they will make the initial introductions, make sure everyone is on the same page, and then let you (the photographer) take the lead.

HAVE THE RIGHT EQUIPMENT (AND BACKUPS!)

Go with me here: you finally snag your dream job. You're shooting a fashion editorial on location in New York City. You've done the location scouting. You've communicated clearly with your point of contact. And you've come up with a game plan to ensure you get "the shot." You get your equipment set up, the subject arrives and gets in position, and everyone is looking at you expectantly to get started...only for your camera battery to die. You dig frantically through your bag for your backup, but it's nowhere to be found. While this is every photographer's worst nightmare, it can be avoided. A key part of this pre-work phase is making sure you have all the equipment you need: batteries fully charged, backups for days, and any additional gear you've requested or rented ahead of time. You're asking questions early and often, and not waiting until the day of the shoot to request those things. That's a no-no! Remember your mantra? *Hope for the best and prepare for the worst.*

Of course, things can still go wrong. But that's where soft skills—like the ability to pivot, problem-solve, come up with a plan of action, and create magic under pressure—come into play. But more on these soft skills later. For now, focus on meticulous preparation to set yourself up for success.

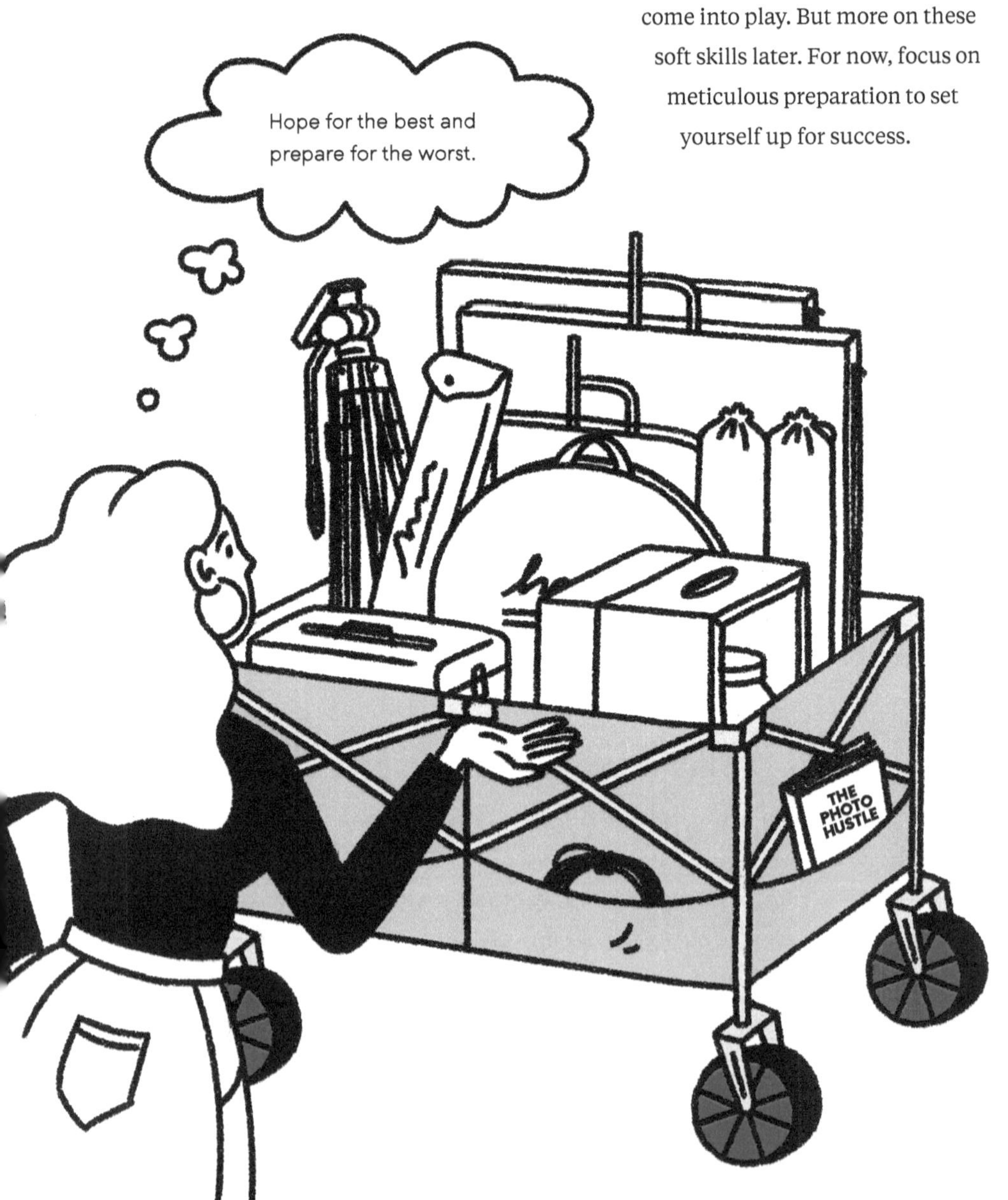

PRODUCTION

Now that you've done your pre-work, it's time to jump into the next phase of the shoot: production. Production encompasses everything that happens on the actual day of the photoshoot. It's when you meet your subject, get the set and location ready, ensure that everyone feels comfortable, and start getting those deliverables you were hired for.

Spoiler alert: things may not go according to plan, but because you've done your due diligence and have a game plan, you know what to do when the worst-case scenario happens. Remember those soft skills I mentioned earlier? This is when you'll need them the most. You're expected to stay calm under pressure and remain professional, no matter how chaotic things get. No one wants to see their photographer running around frantic and flustered, acting like a diva, or being unpleasant just because things didn't go according to plan. When we hire you, we're hiring a professional, and as a professional, you've got to be on top of your game.

On some shoots, you might have a situation where the talent shows up twenty minutes late, or they're really difficult to work with. The photographers who get hired repeatedly have a superpower—they are the ones who can turn a difficult situation around, getting that elusive shot...even when the subject isn't "feeling it."

For larger shoots, it's a little more complex, depending on the type of shoot. Say you're shooting a campaign for an automotive brand, and you're on location at a beach or in the middle of the desert. No matter the conditions, you've got to figure out a way to put those superpowers to use.

You want to make sure you get there early so you are on time for the set. You might be like, "Okay, I arrived early but I'm still waiting five hours later because talent still hasn't shown up yet." That's just part of the gig. Sometimes talent, especially celebrities, have their own timetables. Maybe the shoot is scheduled for 8:00 a.m. and they show up at 4:00 p.m. The two hours you thought you had to get the perfect shot has been cut down to fifteen minutes (including hair and makeup). As hard as that is, you *still* have to be on top of your game!

You, as the photographer, have to dig into those soft skills—and sometimes, it may feel like you're digging *really* deep to find your patience. Remain calm, make sure you're communicating what you need to the producer, photo editor, or art director on set, and give possible solutions instead of complaints. I can tell you this: complaining is the fastest way to get onto the blacklist—but more on that later.

You just want to make sure you're keeping an even temper and going with the flow. That's your job: prepare, then go with the flow and be willing to pivot when things hit the fan.

> **A NOTE FROM KAREN:**
>
> I'm sorry to burst your bubble, but sometimes working with a company or brand means giving up some creative freedom and control. There are very few photographers in the world who get to "do whatever they want" on the job. Remain open to the process and understand that when you're going into this brand, you're working for them, and they are expecting a result that represents their brand. It's not your brand, it's not my brand, it's not anyone else's brand; it's the visual guidelines, it's "The Brand." Don't try to change the brand because the brand will win—every single time.

WHAT ARE SOFT SKILLS?

A great photographer isn't just great because they can take a great photo or have a cutting-edge visual eye. They're great because they have people skills, they know how to communicate well on set, and they're great at problem-solving. And in this industry, there can be a *lot* of problems that come up on set. A great photographer knows how to put out fires and pivot to get the shots they need—while keeping everyone in the room at ease and comfortable. These soft skills are often the very things that elevate a great photographer to the next level…and keep industry insiders like me wanting to work with them again and again. As a photo editor, that's something I'm always looking for when I'm hiring a photographer. Someone might give me a referral for a photographer by saying, "Everything went to crap, but the photographer made something out of nothing." *That's* the person I want to hire.

Soft skills aren't always innate, but they can be learned. You may not be able to get a degree in active listening or problem-solving, but both of those skills can be learned through experience. And you can push yourself to grow in these areas over time. For example, if you're an extreme introvert and talking to a lot of people or speaking in front of a group of people is your worst nightmare, that's okay! You don't have to be an extrovert to be a great photographer. But you can learn how to communicate clearly and effectively to a roomful of people by doing it. The more reps you get in, the better you'll become.

Here are the soft skills that take any photographer from good to great.

Listening

The best photographers I know are exceptional listeners. They truly understand the client's needs. They pick up on unspoken desires and adapt their own personal and artistic style to fit the project at hand. If listening isn't your strongest skill, now is the time to start working on it. Ask more questions in client meetings, pay attention to body language, and repeat back what you hear to make sure you're on the same page. Reading between the lines is also crucial, as sometimes clients might not explicitly say what they want. Follow up to ensure the client is satisfied and that the direction you're taking is in line with their expectations. Remember, your camera captures images, but your ears capture opportunities. Listening carefully not only helps you deliver the best results but also builds trust with your clients, which can lead to repeat business and strong long-term relationships.

Communication

I've mentioned this one a few times already, but that's because I believe it's so important. The best photographers are also the best communicators! Communication goes hand-in-hand with listening, and I believe that the more you communicate, the better everyone's experience on set will be. Don't wait to share important information with your point of contact, the talent, or even your team. The more you communicate, the more seamlessly the shoot will go—and at the end of the day, that's what we all want.

Emotional Intelligence

This one can be a tough skill to learn, especially if it doesn't come naturally to you—but it's not impossible. Being an emotionally intelligent photographer means knowing if the shoot is working at any given moment. As the photographer, you need to know when it's time to say, "We need to do something else to get that shot."

Accepting Constructive Criticism and Feedback

Sometimes, your point of contact may not love the direction the shoot is going in. It's your job to make the client happy and turn in a deliverable that exceeds their expectations. Your photo director may ask you to pivot mid-shoot—and that has to be okay! Taking their constructive criticism well and using their feedback to pivot in the right direction will be a game changer for the rest of the shoot.

Problem-Solving and Adaptability

Have you gotten sick of the words "problem-solving" yet? If not, I'm sure you will. It's one of the most important soft skills you can have as a photographer. You don't have to have the answers for *everything*, but you do need to be able to come up with solutions quickly—and on the spot. Problem-solving and being adaptable means offering up alternative options and solutions instead of complaining. Complaining is one of the first things that can land you on the blacklist—more on that in Chapter 9.

A NOTE FROM KAREN:

Clients don't just hire you to click a button. They hire you to be a professional who can meet deadlines, work within budgets, collaborate effectively, handle unexpected challenges, and deliver results that exceed their expectations. When you focus on developing these soft skills alongside your creative abilities as a photographer, there's no ceiling to what you can do with your career.

WHO'S ON SET?

Let me start by sharing that every photoshoot and every set is different, depending on the desired outcomes. The people you'll find on set will vary with which side of the industry you're working with: brand or editorial. Then, the type of shoot also plays a big role—whether it's food, fashion, automotive, etc. The bigger and more complicated the shoot, the more people you'll typically have on set.

If it's an editorial shoot and the subject is not a notable person, usually no one is on set. You may just have the photo director/editor or an art director. Many times, it's up to you to make plans with the subject and get the shoot done independently. However, if you're working on a big celebrity cover for a magazine, you're probably going to see the editor-in-chief on set as well. Sometimes, it's the only time an editor can interview the subject—and you'll all have to work together to pull it off.

If you're working with a brand on a campaign and the subject is notable, you'll often see the photo director and both the photo lead and creative director. Additionally, on the brand side, you may be working with a producer, a photo editor, and an art director, and sometimes even the creative director is on set. You could also have a crew of DigiTechs and photo assistants, depending on the scale of the shoot. The larger the project, the more people are involved, and understanding your role in relation to the team will help everything run smoothly.

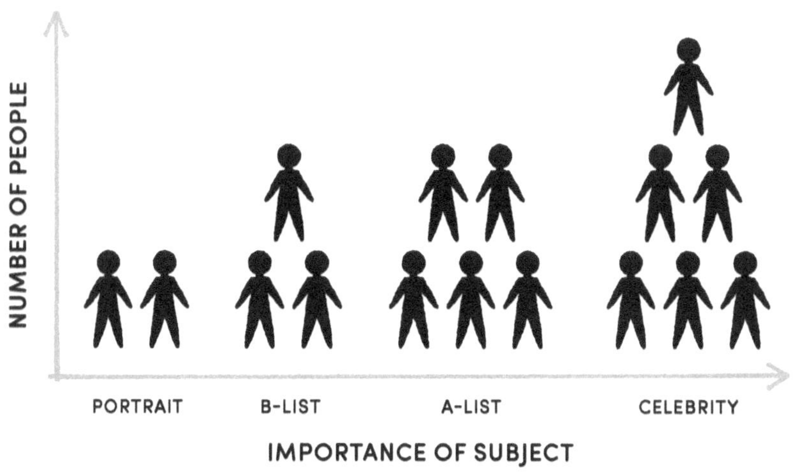

HOW TO BEHAVE ON SET

As the photographer, your number one goal is meeting your deliverables while creating a positive environment and experience for everyone on set. In photography, you'll sometimes work with amazing crews. Other times, you may find yourself with a less-than-ideal team. You just never know what you're going to get until you get there. You know what they say: sometimes, the only thing you can control is you. So, knowing how to maintain professionalism while dealing with a lot of moving parts, people, and personalities will serve you well in the long run and help ensure you get hired again and again.

Years ago, I was working as a virtual art director for a company on a photoshoot. Let me tell you: the subject was a pain in the butt. They were very rude, and when it was time for the photographer to do their thing, the subject actually said, "F—k you!" and walked right off the set. I wasn't on set myself, but I was directing the shoot virtually and received a frantic text from the photographer sharing what happened. At this point, I had to make sure the photographer was okay while collaborating with the producer to ensure the shoot would still go on. (Did I mention this was planned as a two-day shoot with a specific number of deliverables?) Fortunately, the photographer was fine, remaining calm and professional. The producers on set handled the situation, talked to the publicist, and made it clear that we still needed to get the images, no matter what. At the end of the day, the subject came back, and we were able to continue the shoot and get what we needed. To this day, I give mad props to the photographer for handling such a difficult situation with so much grace.

Sadly, these types of challenges aren't rare in the world of photography. That's why it's so important to have the people skills and problem-solving abilities it takes to pivot and still get the job you were hired to do done. What the photographer did so well was to remain rational, continuing the shoot despite the difficult circumstances. However, if they had decided they didn't want to continue, I would have completely understood. We would've found another photographer to take their place or found another solution to get the job done. At the end of the day, we *have* to get the deliverables. In my position, I always try to find a way to make sure the photographer feels comfortable and supported, which often includes prioritizing safety on set.

SAFETY ON SET

As the photographer, you have every right to feel safe on set. If there's ever a time when you don't feel safe, it's important to share your concerns with your producer, art director, or creative director. Just pull them aside and let them know what happened and why you're not comfortable continuing with the shoot. It's their job to make sure you feel safe and have everything you need to do your job effectively. After all, it's hard to do a good job when you're uncomfortable on set.

We all strive for a positive experience on set, and sometimes that just doesn't happen. If something goes wrong, it's important to address it after the shoot in a postmortem meeting. This is where you can document the incident and run it up the right flagpole so the appropriate actions—or consequences—can be taken.

Hear me out: do not ever feel like you need to stay silent for fear of losing out on a gig. If something happens that makes you feel uncomfortable or unsafe, it's essential that you approach your point of contact respectfully and let them know what happened. It's their responsibility to help resolve the situation so you can continue working safely and professionally. Ultimately, it's up to you to decide where your boundaries are. If something happens that makes you feel unsafe—whether physically or emotionally—and you can't continue the shoot, it's okay to step away. Just make sure to communicate with the right people so they can help find a solution that ensures both your safety and the success of the shoot.

POST-PRODUCTION

Hopefully, you experienced a great photoshoot and showed everyone on set how amazing you are at problem-solving, communicating, and commanding the room. Now that the shoot is over, you can start working on those deliverables you promised. Depending on what you agreed to in the contract, you may have to deliver the raw, untouched images (.raw or RAW files) or begin the retouching process. If you're working with an editorial company, they might just want your favorite selection of photos taken during the shoot. Once chosen, you'll deliver the hi-res versions to their editorial team to use for the project. If your shoot was with a brand or company, those deliverables may look different depending on your agreement. Maybe they want you to deliver the full take of RAW images for them to sort through and select. Or maybe they want you to deliver a large selection of your favorites and begin the retouching process once they make their selections. If you agreed to a complete buyout, you'll be handing over every single image you took, and boom, you're done. But just because your deliverables are completed doesn't mean the job is fully wrapped up. You've still got to get paid, right?!

INVOICING

The last thing you want is for the brand or magazine to chase you down for your invoice before they can pay you. Turn that baby in as soon as you can, no matter if you're net 30, net 60, or net 90. The sooner you can get that to us, the sooner you get paid. In the brand space, you'll typically submit your invoice to the photo editor or director, who will then pass it off to the accounting team. After they review and approve it, the invoice is processed, and your payment is on its way. But if there are any mistakes on the invoice, this can lengthen the process and delay payment. Keep in mind that your payment date starts from when the invoice is submitted and approved by the finance team, not from the day of the shoot. Most photographers are great at submitting invoices promptly (because they want to get paid!). And others are forgetful—that goes for our side of things as well. We're all human!

Once you turn in your invoice and get paid, the job is done. The hope is that you'll hear from your photo editor or another point of contact from the magazine or brand. But if your inbox is nothing but crickets, it could be a sign that the shoot didn't go as well as expected. You may have just landed yourself on the blacklist. If that's the case, it's not the end of the world. In Chapter 9, I'm going to share everything you need to know about the dreaded blacklist: how you got there, how to get off, and how to clear your name—for good.

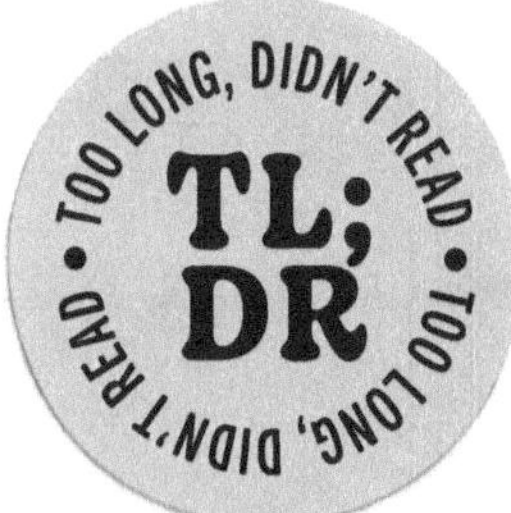

- Your new mantra for *every* photoshoot needs to be, "Hope for the best and prepare for the worst." You may think that sounds cheesy, but I promise it'll serve you shoot after shoot.

- Location scouting, communicating well, and making sure you have *all* your equipment primed and ready to go are all necessary parts of pre-production. Don't skip any of these steps!

- Come up with a game plan for the shoot ahead of time — and expect it to go wrong. Learning to pivot will be your superpower in this industry.

- Soft skills are what will get you hired again and again. Learning how to use them and putting them into action will take you from good to great.

- Be on your best behavior. It's your job as the photographer to make sure everyone is comfortable and has what they need for the shoot to go smoothly.

- Feeling safe on set isn't just a good idea. It's your right. Never be afraid to speak up for yourself!

- Turn in your deliverables (early or on time) and get your invoice to your point of contact as soon as you can. You want to get paid, don't you?

- If your inbox is crickets after the job, you may have landed yourself on the blacklist. In the next chapter, I'll share what you did to get there and how you can clear your name.

CHAPTER 9

The BLACKLIST. *It's Real.*

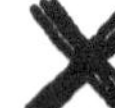

*"Photography is a very small world,
and for photographers, reputation is currency."*

—BLACK VISUAL QUEEN

You've heard whispers about it. You've dreaded the idea of ever finding your name on it. You've also gaslighted yourself into believing it's all just a myth. I hate to break it to you: there *is* a blacklist...and it's *very* real.

If you've been shooting for editorial and brands for a while and are suddenly experiencing tumbleweeds in your inbox—you may want to start paying attention. If your email was full of booking requests and your calendar was constantly full, but now you can't seem to get a gig no matter how hard you try, you may be on the dreaded blacklist.

WHAT IS THE BLACKLIST?

To put it bluntly, the blacklist is a "s—t list" of photographers created by brand and editorial industry insiders (think photo directors and editors, producers, and art directors). It's a list meant to warn other industry professionals about who to hire and who to steer clear of. As a photographer, you may have heard of the blacklist before, and there's probably a good number of stories that surround it. Let me start by clearing a few things up.

THERE'S NO "MASTER" BLACKLIST

It's important to understand that there isn't just one universal "master" blacklist that everyone in the industry shares access to. Different brands, publications, and production companies all maintain their own blacklists. These lists vary in format, organization, and level of detail, and I've seen quite a few of them throughout my career. Some are meticulously color-coded with the color red, meaning, "Do *not* hire," yellow signifying "Proceed at your own risk," and green meaning "Would hire again."

Other lists I've seen give lengthy explanations with details of the job, what went wrong, and why a certain photographer should never be hired again. Then, some lists are more straightforward, with just names and a few notes about what happened on set.

No matter the format, being on the blacklist can seriously harm your reputation, so it's important to remain professional, reliable, and easy to work with so you'll never find yourself on one.

IT'S ALL SUBJECTIVE

I'm not trying to be all doom and gloom here. It's important to keep in mind that these blacklists are not set in stone—they're very subjective. For example, you might have had a less-than-ideal experience working with someone, but that same person might be on someone else's speed dial. If I am being asked for photographer recommendations and see someone asking about a photographer who may be on my personal blacklist, I may raise a flag and be like, "Hey, you can work with this photographer, but I want you to know the context. Here are some red flags you need to be aware of."

Getting off on the wrong foot with one person can lead to them refusing to ever give you another chance again. However, if you hit it off with another person, they might still refer you, even if your name is on another person's list. The hiring process is never just about one person's opinion. Often, there are multiple decision-makers. So, while you might be on one person's blacklist, another person might recognize you were just having a bad day and want to give you a second chance. But in cases where a senior figure, like an art director or editor-in-chief, has decided they won't work with you again, their decision will likely outweigh any other opinions.

Remember, everyone has their own level of tolerance for working with others. In fact, I've had terrible experiences with some photographers throughout my career. Remember the time I got bamboozled? That photographer made it very difficult to communicate on set when I needed to. After I moved to another company and position, that same photographer tried to hit me up for more work. But because my experience was so awful, I didn't even respond. So, if you think that your name may be in the clear because that one difficult photo editor moved to a different role, they'll still remember. Unfortunately, you don't get a fresh slate.

IT'S NOT PERMANENT

The good news is that being on the blacklist isn't necessarily permanent. Unless something illegal or truly morally reprehensible happens, most experiences don't result in a permanent ban. A single bad shoot won't automatically put you at the top of someone's list of people they refuse to work with. However, if something does go wrong and you don't handle it well, you'll need to work hard to rebuild trust with that person, crew, or brand.

When you're on set, you need to make sure you're hyperaware of your behavior and actions. Maintaining professionalism at all times, especially when things don't go as planned, can go a long way in preventing lasting damage to your reputation. Once trust has been rebuilt, and the situation can be explained as an isolated incident or a fluke, people will often be open to giving you another chance, and those referrals will start coming in again.

EVERYONE TALKS

Listen closely: your reputation follows you *everywhere*. So, if you do something on a set that has major implications, you have to trust that it *will* get out to other people—especially in this industry. No matter what you do in this world, your reputation travels with you. And in this industry, everyone talks. There's a network of industry insiders who share information about photographers with each other. There are even secret groups where we give each other referrals, provide recommendations, and search for the latest scoop on the best and worst photographers to work with.

It's not just one-sided, either. Early in my career, I learned this valuable lesson the hard way. I was on set and wasn't being the most professional version of myself. After the shoot, I received some constructive feedback from my team and crew members, reminding me that there are eyes and ears *everywhere*—and you never know who is listening. It could be a friend of the editor-in-chief, a cousin, or a coworker who is closely connected to someone higher up in the industry. No matter who it is, word gets around—*fast*. I'm grateful for that lesson because my lack of professionalism on set could've cost me future work and opportunities. The same holds true for you—especially as a freelance photographer. The creative industry is a small world, and it's easy to think that if you make a mistake on set, no one will notice. But trust me, they will. People are always sharing recommendations. Someone might bring up your name and someone else might chime in with, "Do not work with this person. They were unprofessional on set."

There's a saying that goes, "You're only as good as your last job." But you're also only as bad as your worst job. I repeat: your reputation is everything. If you *know* you have the talent, you're getting the work done, and the economy is good, but you're still not getting hired…you may have to do some inventory. Ask yourself, "Am I a pleasant person to work with? Am I bringing drama to the set? Did I make someone uncomfortable?" If you answered "Yes" to any of these questions, you may be on the blacklist.

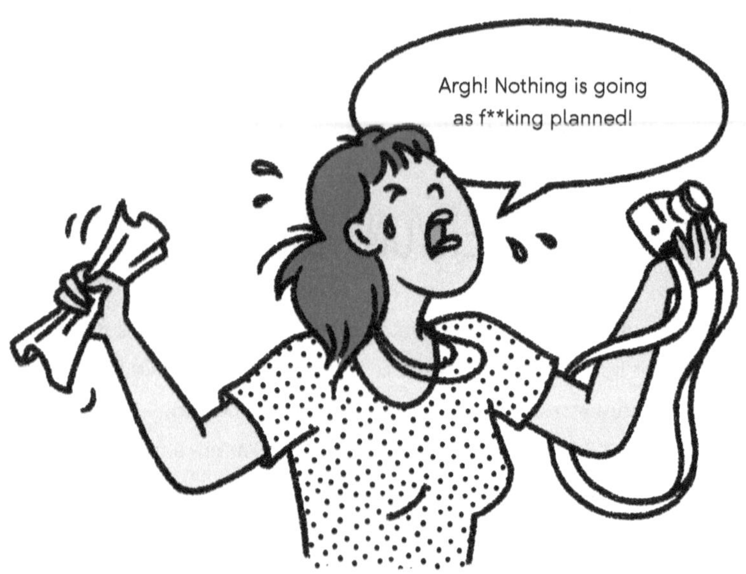

HOW TO GET *ON* THE BLACKLIST

One of the fastest ways to land yourself on the blacklist is by being unpleasant to work with. Nobody enjoys collaborating with someone who is pushy, hard to deal with, doesn't communicate well, or—worst of all—overpromises and under-delivers. However, these traits alone won't necessarily put you straight on the blacklist. I've worked with some photographers that I hate being in the same room with…but I continue to work with them because they under-promise and over-deliver. Mastering this skill will take you far in your career—no matter what your field is!

If you show up to a shoot with a big ego, act like a diva, or cause drama, no one will want to hire you again. Think about all the people you've had the opportunity to collaborate with in your life: if someone is pushy, rude, dramatic, or just straight-up toxic, you're probably not jumping at the chance to work with them again, right? The same is true for this industry. I've worked at places with lists that said, *"Do not contact under any circumstances."* If the talent requested that person, we've had to redirect them to a different photographer.

As a photographer, you're hired not only for your unique visual eye and creativity but also with the expectation that you're going to show up humble, kind, professional, flexible, and willing to do whatever it takes to get the job done. If you're having a bad day, that's okay—we're all human, and bad days are normal. But being a professional means learning how to leave all of that at the door. Don't let your bad days, bad attitudes, or big ego get in the way of your competence. Especially if this is your first time working with a new company, brand, publication, or client, you don't have the relational trust built up yet. These people don't know you, your work, or your personality. That's why you must show up with your game face on, pulling out all those soft skills you've mastered. Because whether this is your first job or your eight-hundredth, you *still* have to hustle.

INSIDER TIPS:

"The thing that would deter me most from working with a photographer again is someone who brings ego to the set and thinks that their needs are more important than the clients'. A great on-set experience is never one-sided, so collaboration and good set vibes are paramount to a great outcome."

— CHRISTINA COOKSEY, FOUNDER OF CEILING TRAIN

"If a photographer has too much of an ego, I do not want to work with them."

— JENNIFER PERLMUTTER, SENIOR PHOTO AND MOTION REPRESENTATIVE

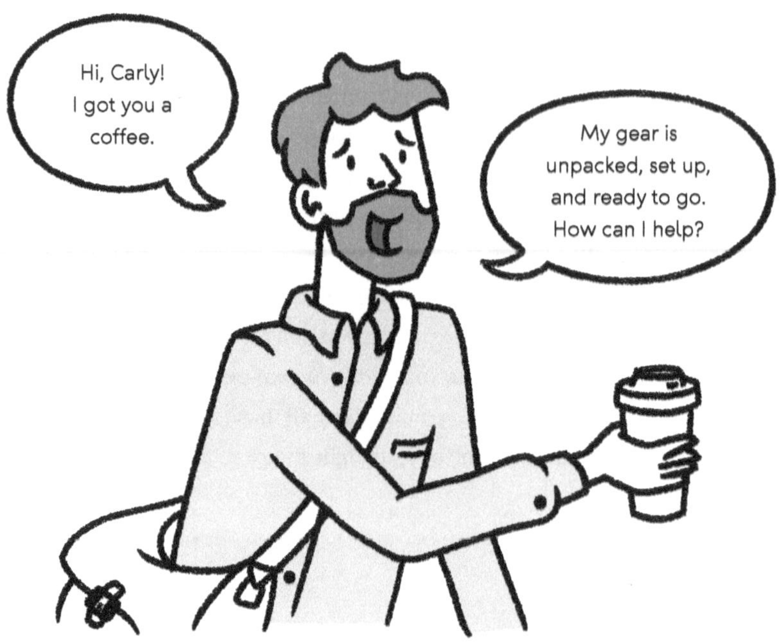

HOW TO GET *OFF* THE BLACKLIST

Here's the deal: one bad experience, one off-day on set, or one tough gig doesn't keep you on the blacklist forever. Does being on the blacklist mean you're doomed to never work again? No, not at all!

Some photographers on the list have still been getting work to this day. Remember, these lists are *subjective*. What one person may be willing to tolerate, another might not, and that includes how they view your skill, experience, and talent level. Sometimes being on the blacklist simply means "room for improvement." And part of being a professional means being able to take criticism and feedback—and then making the necessary changes to improve. People will respect you for owning your mistakes, learning from them, and showing that you're capable of evolving. By demonstrating that you can adapt, you'll be well on your way to rebuilding trust and earning back those opportunities.

INSIDER TIPS:

"A photographer who is calm and collected, who keeps their cool and is able to pivot when things don't go exactly as planned, is a great photographer to work with. A partner and collaborator is the type of photographer I'll bring back again and again. I'm always looking for a photographer who has outstanding standards for creative delivery and is willing to get it right, but is also partnership-oriented and willing to collaborate with the agency/clients."

— CHRISTINA COOKSEY, FOUNDER OF CEILING TRAIN

"I like a photographer who collaborates with their crew and lets their individual strengths shine. We all work together."

— JENNIFER PERLMUTTER, SENIOR PHOTO AND MOTION REPRESENTATIVE

"I believe in positivity, collaboration, and preparation to make a shoot come together seamlessly. If a photographer is unprepared, or simply difficult and refuses to listen to a client or adjust during the shoot, it could leave a bad lasting impression."

— FRANCESCA GALESI, DIRECTOR OF PHOTOGRAPHY AT ATEDGE

YOU *CAN* REDEEM YOURSELF!

In this industry, no one wants to burn bridges. People in my position want to create lasting and fruitful relationships with great photographers we can trust to cover our projects again and again. And on the photographer's side, I know you want the same thing.

Listen, we're not in the business of ruining people's lives; we all want to make a living making art—that's our collective goal. I know you're an awesome photographer. You're kind, you're humble, you go with the flow, you're not a pushover, you have emotional intelligence, you know how to read a room, and, best of all, you over-deliver. That is what is going to get you off the list. That's how you get into the rhythm of repeat clients who love working with you. Make it easy on us! And in return, we can make it easy on you.

Even if you're on the blacklist, you can still redeem yourself. No one is perfect, and everyone deserves a second chance. I've seen photographers turn over a new leaf and continue to work and make beautiful art. On set, they're professional, they get the job done, they're communicative, and they deliver the work on time. They've course-corrected, stayed flexible, and checked their egos at the door. I've personally taken photographers off the blacklist because they've matured and improved over time.

That's not to say that you don't have your own version of a blacklist for people, companies, and publications on our side of the industry. Believe me, we can be a-holes too, making it difficult for you to do the job you were hired to do! But when you keep your cool and stay flexible, people will see that you can handle this weird, sometimes toxic environment. The bottom line? Make it easy for people. Make them feel seen and heard. Show up, be professional, and you won't ever have to worry about a blacklist.

Oh, and another thing: learn how to separate yourself from the work you do—especially if you're working with brands. Developing this skill early in your career will help you stay professional, no matter what the job is.

LEARN HOW TO DETACH

One of the hardest things to do as a creative is to detach yourself from your work. Photography is taught at a very personal level. You're making personal work, you're putting your all into it, and you're producing an image unique to you. Those are all good things and are a big part of why people love the art so much. But it's also the root of what causes photographers (and even photo editors) to get themselves into trouble.

When I was a "baby" photo editor, I was tasked with doing a select from a wide edit. In my mind, the images I chose were the absolute *best*. However, the person requesting the work decided to go in a completely different direction. I was *crushed*. "Why would they pick this photo for the cover when this is *clearly* the best one?" It took me years before I learned the beauty of detaching from my work. Now, I'm able to ask myself the question, "Is this a hill I need to die on?" While my job on this side of the industry is to pick the best images from any given shoot, it's often someone else who makes the final decision. And I have to live with that.

There will always be images you create that will be personal to you. But when you're getting paid by a brand or client to work on *their* project, they ultimately have the final say. There will be times when you do an entire photoshoot, and the client or brand decides not to use any of those images. Maybe they decided to pivot, go a different direction, or the project gets cut completely. I know it stings. I know it hurts. Just remember: always remain professional. *Everyone sees everything.*

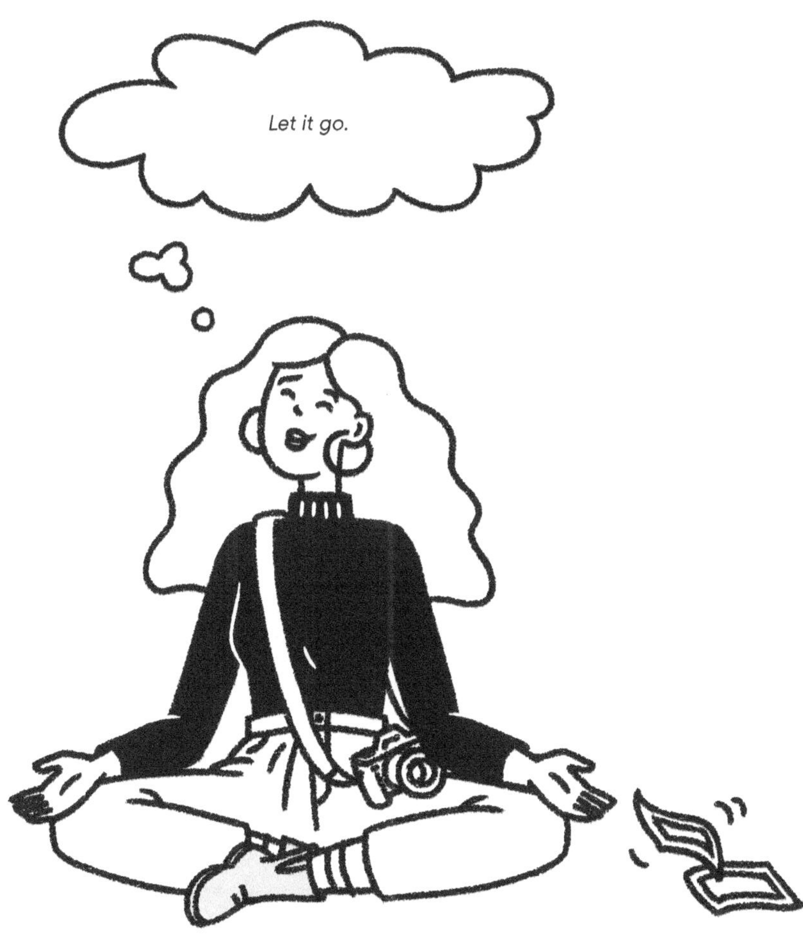

A NOTE FROM KAREN:

Sometimes, the frustration of a job gone wrong can get the best of you. Over the years, I've seen photographers vent their frustration from a job on social media. Hear me out: as a photographer (and a human), you're free to say whatever you want. But when you call people, brands, or publications out on your social media…everyone sees it. And when you do, you're choosing to burn bridges. When you air your grievances in a public way, it never looks good on you as

a photographer. It may even affect your ability to get future work. Other producers, other art directors, and other stakeholders are looking at that. And if they're seeing you call out another company, they're not going to hire you for fear that you'll do the same to them as well. Every action has a consequence, positive or negative. The choice is yours.

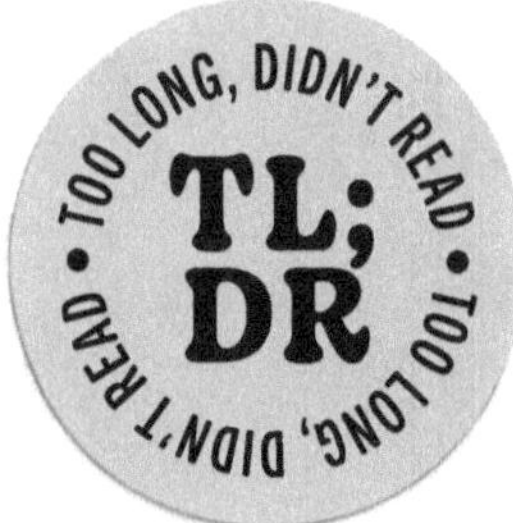

- The blacklist is *real.*

- There is no master list. Sometimes it's a physical list, and other times it's digital. And there's no telling how many lists exist on this side of the industry.

- The blacklist is very subjective. You may be on one person's caution list and on another person's speed dial. The list varies due to each person's experience of working with you.

- You can be removed from the blacklist. It's not permanent. So, if you've been hearing crickets in your inbox after a shoot that went wrong, don't worry. You can redeem yourself!

- It's important to know how to detach yourself from your work. Photography is an art. Therefore, it's very personal. But if someone is paying you to do the work, at the end of the day, it's theirs. Knowing how to let go will take you far!

- Be humble. Be kind. Under-promise and over-deliver. These are the traits that will keep you off the blacklist.

CHAPTER 10

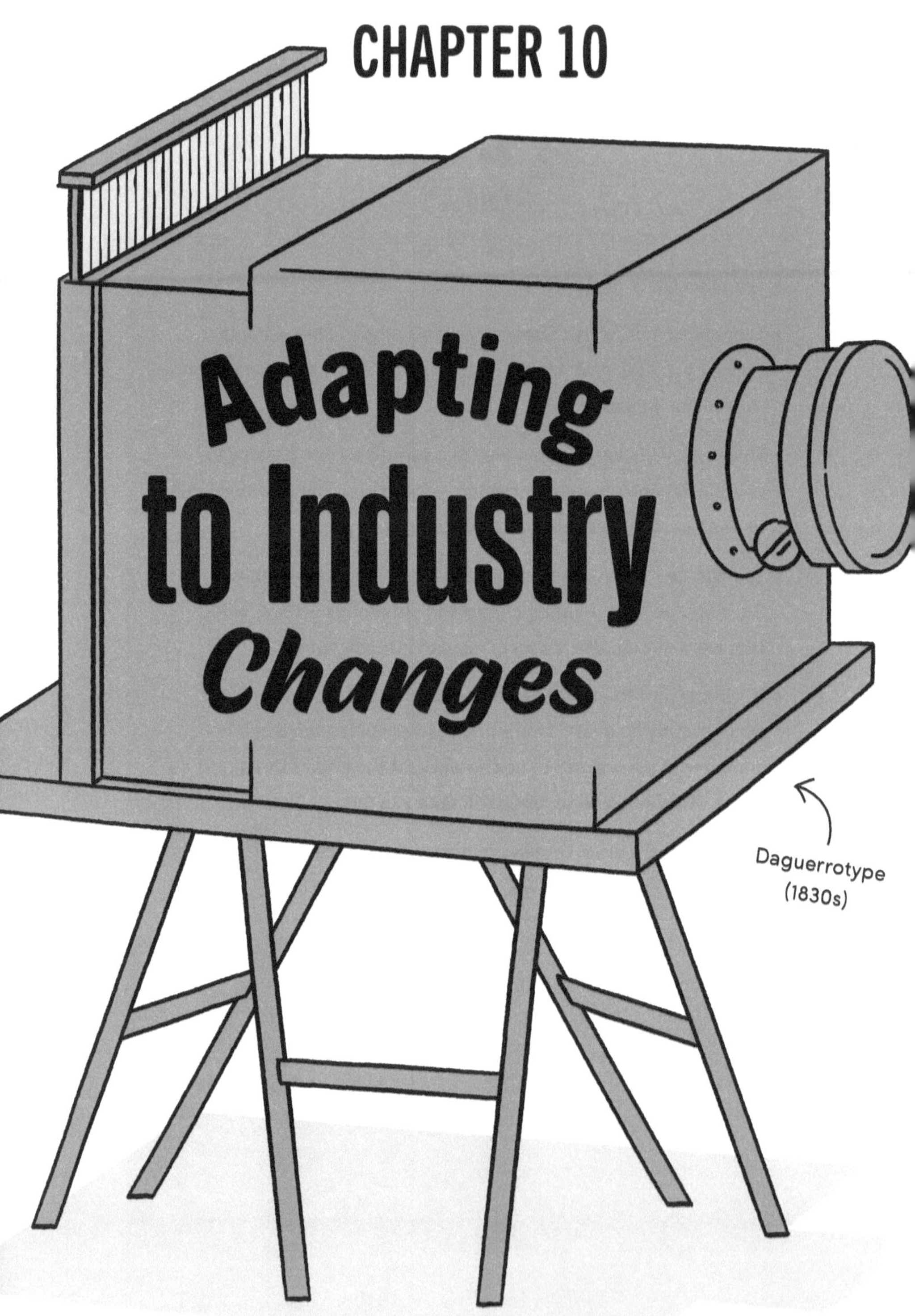

Daguerrotype
(1830s)

"The genie is out of the bottle. AI is the genie... Learn how to make it work for you."

—BLACK VISUAL QUEEN

Times are changing! I wanted to dedicate the last chapter of this book to industry changes, specifically regarding the increasingly popular use of artificial intelligence (AI). Before we dive in, I want you to take a deep breath: it's not as scary as you may think.

TECHNOLOGY IS *ALWAYS* CHANGING

Think about any invention that has moved this country forward that you now use daily without much thought. For instance, you're probably really grateful to have indoor plumbing instead of going outside to use an outhouse multiple times a day. I doubt people are still complaining about that glow-up. But if we're honest, there's always someone resistant to change. When electricity was invented, I'm guessing people were up in arms about using that instead of continuing to use candles for light.

When AI was first introduced, it sparked widespread excitement. Sure, much of the excitement likely stemmed from its novelty. But once people realized that typing in a word, phrase, or question could save them hours of work—they were hooked. However, the honeymoon phase didn't last long. Early adopters quickly discovered that many of the answers AI provided were flawed, ranging from gibberish to outright plagiarism or factual errors. As this new technology evolved through countless iterations, those initial missteps gave way to more accurate and precise responses. Today, there are even jobs out there titled "AI Fact Checker," dedicated to making sure those responses are what they should be.

Technology has propelled us light-years ahead of where we once were. Take photography, for instance: when the camera was first invented, people had to sit still for ten minutes to capture a single shot. Now, you can take countless pictures or videos on your phone or camera in a split second. The evolution of the camera and image processing has been remarkable. From the wet-plate era to the darkroom stage and now into the digital age, the process has become faster, more efficient, and more accessible.

When I was in school, I had the unique opportunity to learn at the intersection of analog and digital photography. Just for perspective: I remember buying Photoshop version two or three in a box from Best Buy—cloud-based software wasn't a thing yet!

Back then, processing images meant spending hours in the wet room. Dodging and burning to adjust light and dark areas was tedious, and color processing was even more challenging. At my school, we didn't develop color film because the process back then was so complex. Instead, we learned how to print color images manually with a tool called Jobo. This required working in *complete* darkness during certain parts of the process. I still remember the day my school introduced the color machine. To say I was grateful is an understatement. Suddenly, instead of manually having to go through all these Jobos to get the print, we could now expose it, put the paper in a darkroom, slide it into a machine, and voilà—it was developed! You didn't have to go through three Jobo sets in complete darkness to get the same result. It was amazing.

LEARN TO PIVOT

As humans, we are naturally resistant to change. We cling to our safety nets, preferring to stay in our lanes, and don't want to be pushed outside of our comfort zones. When we are, it's often with hesitation...and a lot of kicking and screaming. But if the year 2020 taught us anything at all, it was that we must know how to pivot—or, at the very least, be willing to try.

Every new technology is created to address a problem that exists in the world, to make something more efficient. AI is no exception. When it was first introduced, many people believed it would solve all our problems. And while it has certainly made some tasks easier, it's also shown its limitations. That said, AI has come a long way and can now accomplish some pretty incredible things. Listen to me closely: just because AI is here to stay doesn't mean photographers—or any other creatives—are going anywhere.

Think about the writing world. Tools like spellcheck or Grammarly are early, widely used forms of AI. Now, platforms like ChatGPT can help us draft emails, organize our thoughts, and help us refine our word choices. Does this mean that AI will take the place of writers everywhere? Not at all. AI is just a helpful tool for people to use—if they choose. Here's the reality, though: people still crave and deeply value human connection—especially in a post-2020 world. They want authenticity. They don't want to engage with a robot. They don't want fake images. When people look at a photo, they're looking for meaning, emotion, and a sense of connection. That's something no amount of AI can replicate.

EMBRACING AI TECHNOLOGY IN YOUR BUSINESS

On my side of the industry, AI makes it easier to brainstorm ideas. When we're thinking about a set, instead of spending hours on a mood board, we can put in a prompt to generate an idea. But we still need boots on the ground to build out the steps, put together the set, and get the job done.

So, the question becomes: How can you make AI work *for* you instead of against you? How can you utilize it to streamline things in your business? Maybe you use AI to generate ideas for your next photoshoot or to assist with post-production tasks. But a word of caution: don't rely on AI to the point where the image you produce no longer resembles the one you originally captured. If there's concern about AI infiltrating creative spaces without our knowledge, then we, as professionals, must take responsibility. Using AI responsibly means being aware of its limitations. It's crucial not to push false narratives. While AI can be a helpful tool, it's not infallible. No technology is 100 percent accurate or perfect all the time, so it's essential to double-check your output for quality and hard facts.

ALWAYS BE WILLING TO ADAPT

In recent years, videography has become a highly sought-after service in this industry. Photographers are always asking me, "Is everything moving to video?" In my experience, and with the rise of social media platforms, video is becoming a priority over images, especially in the world of brands. That's not to say that photography is going away. There will *always* be a need for still images, but we are moving into a motion-first landscape.

My advice to you? Focus on what you're passionate about. Don't just tack video onto your services to stay relevant. If you say you do videos and you show up on set and your skills are lackluster at best, that's not going to look good. So, if you choose to offer video services, the quality of your motion work needs to match the excellence of your still photography. Don't worry; I'm not telling you to go back to school and get a film degree. Many photographers I know have successfully transitioned into photo directing through hands-on experience and trial and error. They've honed their ability to bring a vision to life through motion and have collaborated with professionals like editors, sound technicians, and colorists to polish their projects. But that doesn't mean you *have* to shoot video to be a successful photographer and get work in today's climate.

No matter what the latest trend is, you must always be willing to grow and learn. Many photographers believe that simply learning how to use their camera and mastering the art of a good portrait is enough to succeed. But that's far from the truth. To thrive in this competitive industry, you must continually push forward, perfecting your craft, embracing new technologies, and expanding your horizons. Don't get

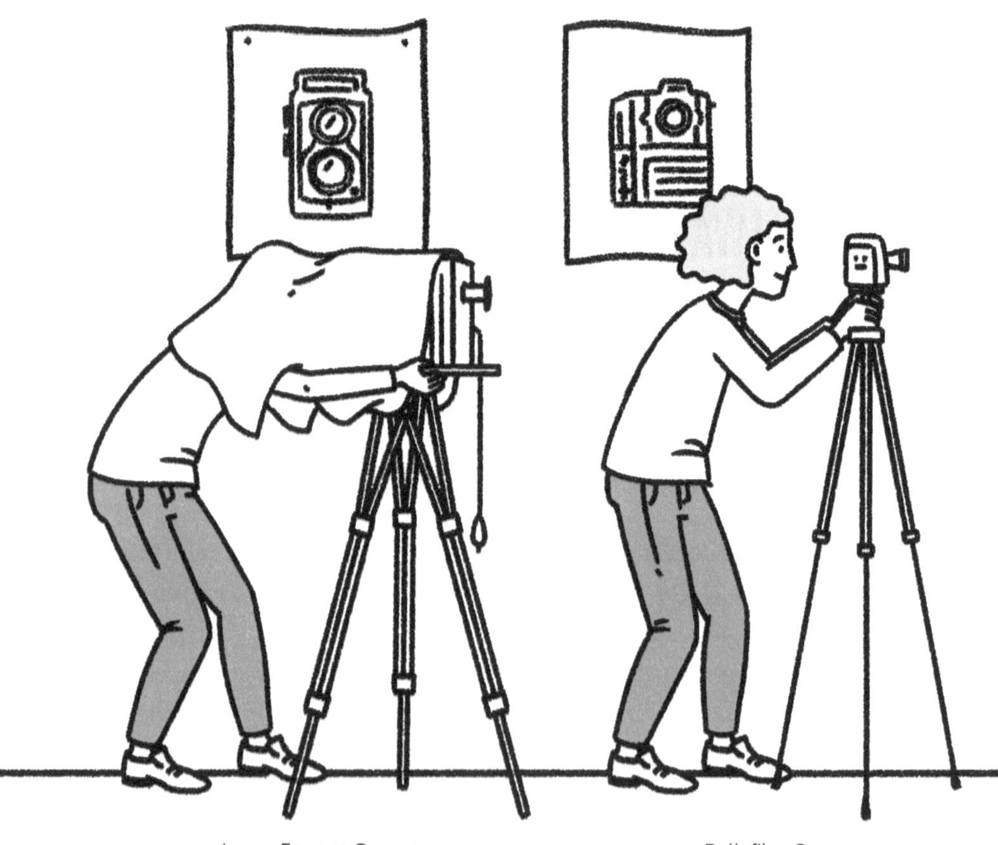

Large Format Camera
(1880s)

Roll-film Camera
(circa 1900s)

stuck—that will kill your business. To stand out, you have to rise above the sea of mediocrity and challenge yourself to do more.

When you're creating and exploring new things, not everything will work. But that's exactly why you do it—so you can learn more about yourself, what you love to create, and what you're good at. Adaptability and a growth mindset will keep you at the top of your game in this ever-evolving industry.

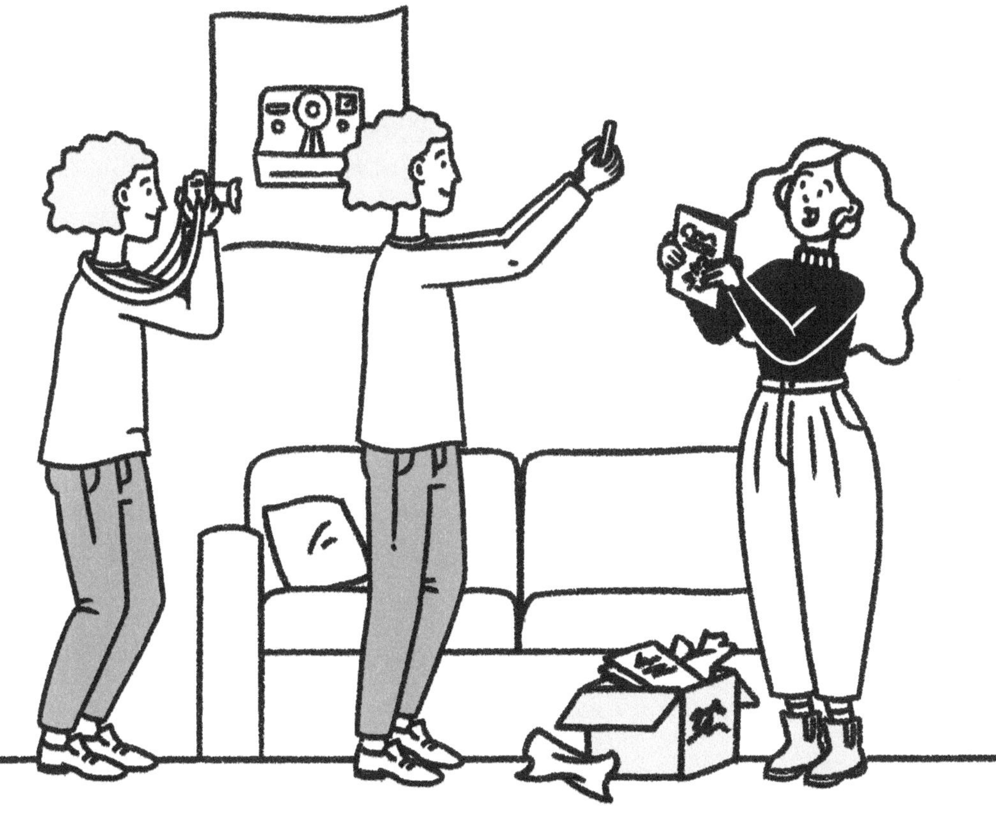

SLR Camera
(1940s)

Cell Phone Camera
(2000s)

A NOTE FROM KAREN:

AI cannot do everything. In this industry, AI exists to help streamline processes and make workflows more efficient—not to replace human photographers. We still need to hire professional photographers like you to take the photos. We still need your visual eye to create these covers, billboards, products, and more that make the world go 'round. People continue to crave, desire, and love the authenticity you bring to the world around you.

Consider the car industry when robots were first introduced to factories. Were some jobs lost? Absolutely. But even those manufacturing plants still rely on human beings to maintain the automated functions and carry out quality control. The same is true for photography. Will jobs be lost? In a sense, yes. But not as many as you might think. AI isn't here to replace photographers entirely. However, it may filter out those photographers who are trying to be all things to all people. This is why finding your niche and honing the unique creativity you bring to the world and the industry is crucial. You must keep learning, growing your skillset, mastering your craft, and leveling up your game. When we look at your portfolio, you can show us that we still need what you bring to the table.

Photography is not dead. It will always be changing and evolving, just as it has been since its inception. Look at how cameras have transformed over the years and how film processing has advanced. While we respect and honor what came before us, we also embrace change and continue to push forward. Throughout it all, one constant remains: the human desire to capture and preserve moments in time through photographs. Nothing will ever replace the magic of that.

FINAL THOUGHTS FOR PHOTOGRAPHERS

By now, you've heard (and probably experienced) just how tough this industry can be. And when you're brand-new, breaking into the editorial and brand spaces can feel like an impossible task. But if I can do it, I know you can, too. Now, the only thing left to do is get after it!

My colleagues in the industry wanted to leave you with some final words of wisdom. I hope they encourage you as you begin your journey:

"Photograph what you want to see out in the world. Don't be overly concerned with trends. If you stay true to your vision, your perspective, and your way of seeing, the right clients will find you."
—Jennifer Perlmutter, senior photo and motion representative

"There are jobs that you do because you love the subject/client, and there are jobs that you do for good money. Hopefully, you have some that are both."
—Rebecca Karamehmedovic, founder and partner at Sway NY

"This is an all-or-nothing competitive career. I believe it is important to go for it, not overthink, and keep shooting."
—Francesca Galesi, director of photography at AtEdge

"Be persistent. Have a partnership mindset. Remember that commercial photography is a translation of a brand's/client's story. Collaboration is key. Have fun on set. Be willing to pivot. Build relationships every day. People work in the creative space because they want to work with other awesome creatives. Bring that collaborative energy to everything you do, and you'll get repeat calls, guaranteed."
—Christina Cooksey, founder of Ceiling Train

"Set your business up first. Being a photographer isn't just about knowing the craft. It's being professional, having an LLC or corporation, and treating your crew like well-liked partners. Do your homework. Don't think you know it all right out of the gate. Be patient with the process... It takes a long time to be successful. Most of all, stay true to yourself and create space for remaining creative—self-care is key!"
—Traci Terrick, owner of Poppy Creative Agency and founder of Focus on Women

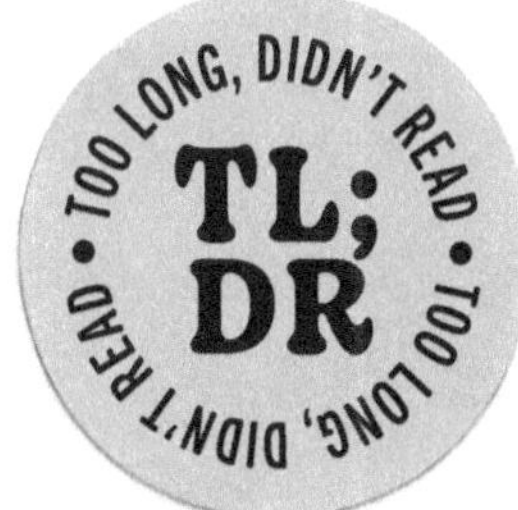

- Technology is a tool that helps us become more efficient in our lives. The introduction of AI is no different.

- AI isn't going to take the place of photography; it's going to expand it.

- AI is a helpful tool that allows you to become more efficient in your business. Don't be fearful of it. Instead, do some research and learn how it can help you in your business, then embrace it.

- Photography isn't dead. It is always growing, changing, and evolving. And as a photographer, you should be too!

- Never stay stagnant. That is the fastest way to kill your business and your relevancy as a photographer. Be willing to learn new things and push yourself outside your comfort zone.

- People will always want to capture a memory or a moment with an image. Photography is here to stay.

CONCLUSION

You're In...
NOW WHAT?

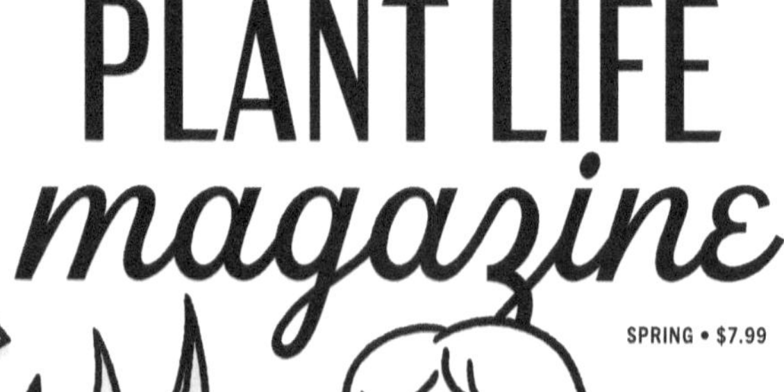

If you're reading this, you've reached the end of our journey together. So...now what? As your self-proclaimed mentor, I get to release you into the world as the badass photographer I know you are. And I hope that after reading this book, you feel more confident, more encouraged, and more empowered, knowing that you *do* have what it takes to "make it" in this industry. I believe in you—now you have to believe in yourself.

As I mentioned at the beginning of this book, I hope this is a valuable resource that you can read and come back to again and again. Keep this book in your camera bag. Dog-ear the pages. Highlight, take notes, and underline the crap out of it. When faced with a new challenge on your business journey, I want you to open this book and think, "There's a chapter for that!"

Before you run off to put all this knowledge into practice, I hope you'll take a beat. Revisit the chapters that align with where you are right now. Soak them in and reflect on what you've read. Take the time to analyze where you're at on this journey. Are you still trying to figure out your why and what you ultimately want to do in photography? Spend some time doing that. Are you ready to market yourself to dream clients? Get to work! Are you trying to get your pitch game together? I hope you'll implement the tips you read. Maybe you've done all that, and you're just wanting to give your skills a glow-up. Whatever stage you're at, you've got this!

Remember, you don't have to go from zero to sixty in a single day. In fact, I advise against it. Progress comes in baby steps, and each one counts. What works for you may not work for the next photographer reading this book. That's why you have to experiment. Try out the tips and suggestions throughout these pages. See what works and what doesn't as you find your footing. Keep learning. Keep taking step after step along your journey to success. Above all, remember that *there is no magic formula*—just your commitment to growth and your passion for the craft.

• • •

Writing this book has been an incredible experience. And if it has helped you on your journey in any way, I'd love to hear about it! Please email me at thephotohustle @gmail.com and share your wins, where you're feeling stuck, and those amazing "aha" moments. I'm here for all of it!

If you've found this book to be helpful, I'd be so grateful if you recommend this to other photographers and creatives. Leave a review on Google and share it with everyone you know. Thank you so much!

Nothing will ever replace the magic of *your* photography!

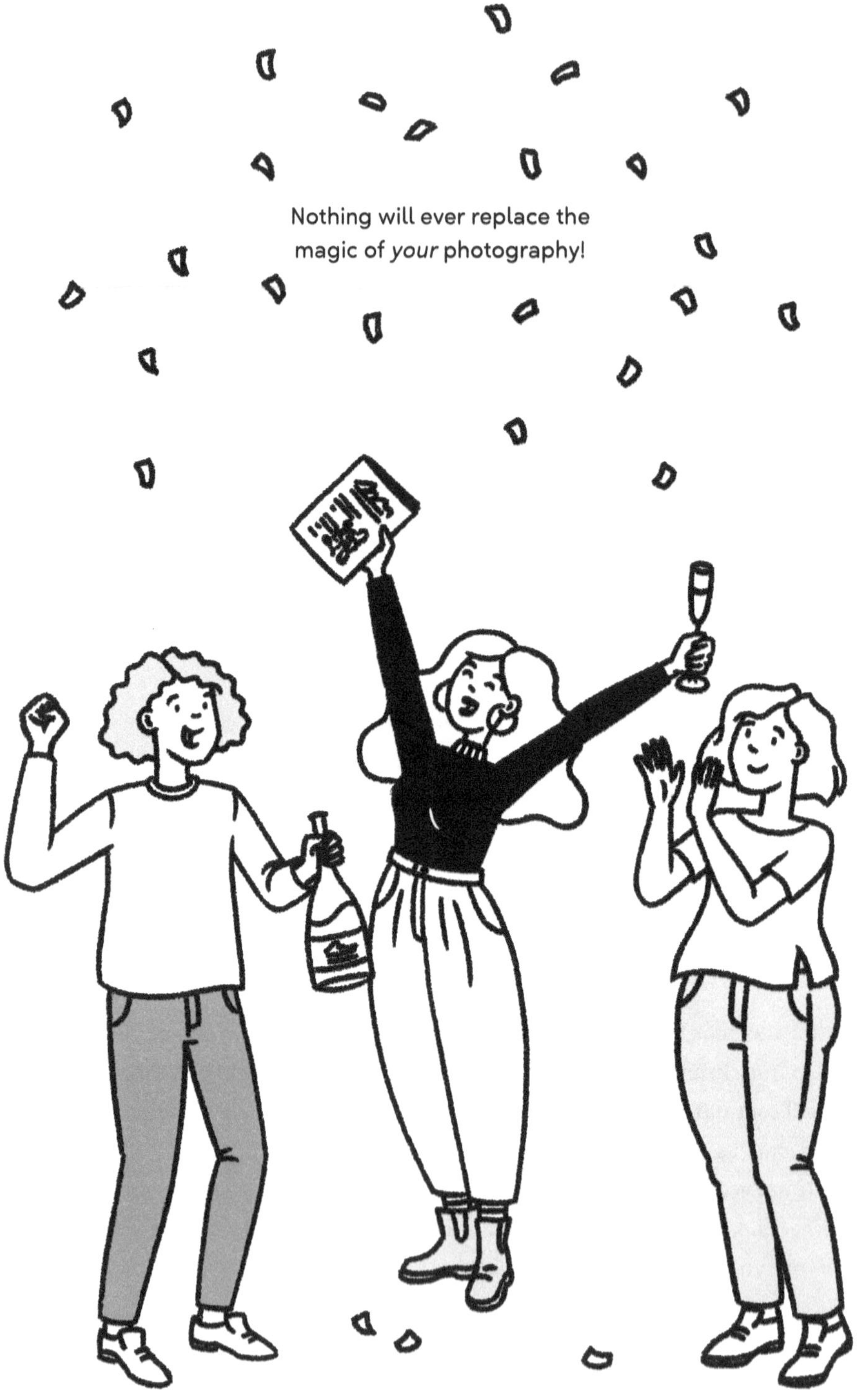

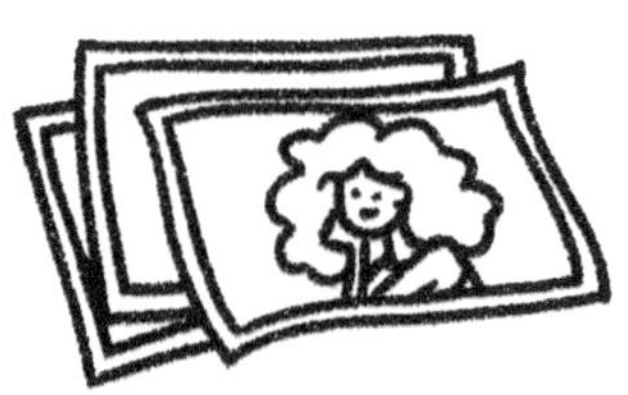

APPENDIX A:

ALTERNATIVE CAREERS FOR PHOTOGRAPHERS

Not all careers in this field involve being a photographer. Here's my list of alternate careers in the visual arts to consider:

Cinematographer:

Often overlooked in discussions about photography, the role of a cinematographer (or director of photography on the photo side) is a vital extension of the craft. On the film side, cinematographers are responsible for the overall visual aesthetic of a project. They collaborate with the director and production designer to shape the lighting, color palette, and camera movements, ensuring the film's look aligns with the creative vision.[17]

Content Creator:

A content creator primarily focuses on written and visual storytelling across various platforms. They generate and curate content for brands, often serving as a jack-of-all-trades for smaller companies. This role may include photography, shooting video, and managing social media content and accounts. Content creators produce a wide range of materials, including blog posts, website articles, social media, videos, graphics, memes, and more, helping brands connect with their audiences creatively and effectively.[18]

Digital Imaging Specialist:

A digital imaging specialist is an expert in preparing digital files for presentation, distribution, and archiving. They make sure that the images are properly organized, sized, colored, and stored. They also ensure the metadata is accurate. This person is responsible for organizing image libraries and tagging images so people can search and find photos easily.[19]

DigiTech:

A DigiTech is the person handling the images taken by a photographer. They make sure they know everything coming in and transfer the data from the camera to the computer. They organize images, back up and label files, and make sure that the presets the photographer had are being properly set. DigiTechs make sure the file delivery of the final product goes smoothly.[20]

Lighting Tech:

Lighting technicians (also known as gaffers or lighting assistants) work closely with the photographer to position the lights in a way that enhances the subjects and achieves the desired composition. They're responsible for setting up lighting equipment and making sure all electrical connections are secure and safe.[21]

Museum Curator Specifically for the Photography Department:

A photo museum gallery curator is a person who researches, collects, and preserves photographs. They're responsible for the archival collection of photos, including their preservation and maintenance within an organization while curating collections from other museums as well.[22]

Photo Agent:

A photo agent specializes in helping photographers book work and build their careers. So, if you thrive on the hustle, love negotiating deals, and enjoy connecting people with opportunities, this role might be perfect for you. Photo agents act as a middleperson between the photographer and the buyer/client. They negotiate sales, help with contracts, and market photographers to their extensive networks.

Photo Art Dealer:

Photo art dealers specialize in buying and selling photographs, often working within the fine art market. They have a keen understanding of the value of photographs and the collectors who are likely to invest in them. Acting as intermediaries, they can assist photographers in selling their work, providing valuable insights into pricing and market trends.

Photo Archivist:

This person is responsible for preserving and organizing historical prints, documents, and other images. They arrange images logically and make them more easily accessible to people who want to view them.[23]

Photo Consultant:

A photo consultant leverages their industry experience to provide expert advice to photographers, brands, businesses, and individuals. This role often involves working freelance to help clients enhance their work, refine their presentation, and develop strategies to land their dream gigs. For example, through my business, Black Visual Queen,

I offer these services to empower photographers to elevate their careers.

Photo Director:

Also known as the director of photography, this person oversees the entire photo department and guides the vision or branding of the entire publication, brand, or campaign, while also handling the logistics of budgets and planning. They also work on high-profile sections of a publication or brand campaign, such as main features and cover stories. This is the most senior-level leader on the photo team.

Photo Editor:

An editorial photo editor selects and oversees the publication of photographs in print or digital media for editorial purposes, for newspapers, magazines, blogs, and websites. They work with photographers, writers, and designers to choose and edit images that best complement written stories. They also manage photoshoots and maintain photo archives, keep track of contracts, use image licenses, and look for copyright infringement and plagiarism.[24]

Photography Instructor:

Instructors teach photography students the technical and creative aspects of photography. They inspire the next generation and give them the tools they need, teaching them everything from how to use a camera and proper lighting to editing and adjusting. Instructors can work at schools or run their own businesses, giving private lessons.

Photo Lab Technician:

A photo lab technician works in a photo lab, developing and printing photographs on the retail side of the industry. At the time of writing this book, photo labs are still around, and people continue to need their photos and films developed and printed. There are also independent photo labs that specialize in these services and are looking for people dedicated to this craft.

Photo Producer:

The photo producer works purely in logistics. They book models and other talent and hire photographers, video developers, and any other crew needed for a successful shoot. They also handle all the contracts, releases, and invoices. Photo producers act as the go-between, making sure a crew has everything it needs and that everything is running smoothly during a shoot. This person is often the first on set and the last to leave, ensuring everything is taken care of.

Photo Studio Manager:

This person is in charge of the day-to-day operations like handling equipment, managing employees, running the studio schedule, and overseeing the budget.[25]

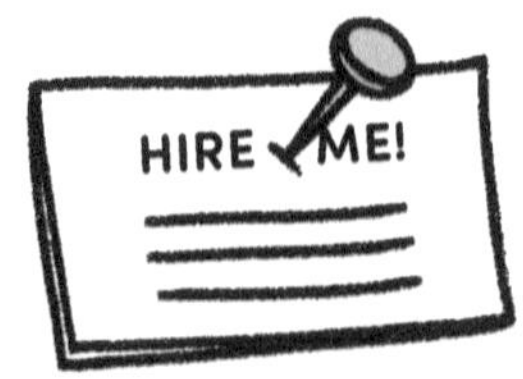

APPENDIX B:

DICTIONARY OF KEY TERMS

Like any profession, the photo industry has its own unique language. Becoming familiar with these commonly used terms will help you navigate the field more effectively. Below are a few key terms to help you on your jargon busting journey. All definitions below are sourced and adapted from APhotoEditor.com and other industry professionals, along with my own industry experience.

Advertising: Images are used in promotional campaigns to market a product. For example, in TV, magazine, or billboard ads.

All Print: Images can be used in all types of print media. For example, in newspapers, brochures, magazines, etc.

Any and All Media: The images can be used across any type of media format. This includes digital, print, broadcast, and more. For example, the use of an image for a digital ad and a print magazine ad.

Attribution: The act of giving credit to the original photographer or copyright holder of an image, often required under certain types of image licenses.

BOB: Back of book. Refers to the final pages of a magazine, often containing the index, final short features, and advertisements.

Book: In the model or photographer context, this refers to a portfolio, a collection of work samples displayed to prospective clients or employers.

Branding: The process of creating a unique identity for your photography business, which includes elements such as your logo, website, and marketing materials. A strong brand helps you stand out from the competition and attracts your ideal clients.

Brief: A set of instructions or guidelines given to a photographer, designer, or artist with specific directions for a job or project.

BTS: Behind the scenes. A look at what goes on during the production of a movie, TV show, or photo shoot, typically not seen by the public.

By Country: Usage specified by individual countries. For example, a global company tailoring its marketing pictures by country due to cultural differences.

Byline: The passionate voice behind the written words of an article, proudly proclaiming their authorship.

Call Sheet: A detailed schedule of a day's shooting for a film or photoshoot.

Call Time: The specific time when talent, crew, and other team members are required to arrive on set for a commercial shoot.

CMS: Content management system. Software that allows users to create, manage, and modify content on a website.

COI: Certificate of insurance. A document issued by an insurance company/broker that is used to verify the existence of insurance coverage.

Collateral: Images used in supplementary promotional materials, like brochures, flyers, etc. Other examples include a product catalog or a college admissions brochure.

Commercial Use: The use of an image for promotional or advertising activities, which can influence sales or the perception of a product, service, or entity.

Commission/Day Rate: The amount of money a person charges for their services for a full day of work. It is a fixed rate for a day's work, rather than an hourly rate, which makes the cost of a day's work vary depending on the number of hours worked.

Consumer: Images used in media aimed at the general public and consumers. For example, use in an e-commerce listing.

Copyright: The exclusive legal right given to a creator or assignee to print, publish, perform, film, or record an artistic work, and to authorize others to do the same. In photography, copyright typically belongs to the photographer who took the image, unless you've signed a contract saying otherwise.

Copyright Infringement: A violation of the rights of the copyright holder, which can involve using, copying, distributing, or displaying a copyrighted work without permission.

Copyright Notice: A note, usually comprising the copyright symbol (©), the year of first publication, and the copyright owner's name, placed on copies of a work to inform the public that the work is under copyright protection.

Corporate: Images used for various corporate purposes such as annual reports, company websites, etc.

Creative Commons (CC): A nonprofit organization that promotes the sharing and use of creative works and knowledge through free, easy-to-use legal tools. They provide a range of customizable copyright licenses that allow creators to retain certain rights while permitting others to use their work under specified conditions.

DAM: Digital asset management. A system that stores, shares, and organizes digital assets in a central location.

Deliverables: The final photographs provided to the client, in digital or physical format.

Derivative Work: A new, original product that contains elements of a copyrighted work. Modifications or edits of a photograph usually constitute derivative work.

Direct Mail: Images used in print advertising sent directly to prospective customers. For example, a photo in a promotional postcard or sales letter.

Digital Millennium Copyright Act (DMCA): A 1998 US law protecting copyrights in the digital age, criminalizing digital rights management (DRM) circumvention and outlining takedown procedures while providing a safe harbor for online platforms.

DMCA Takedown Notice: A notice sent to a service provider, host, or search engine to inform them of copyright-infringing material so they can remove it. This action is protected under the DMCA.

Editorial: Images used in a storytelling context. For example, photos in news articles, blogs, or magazines.

Editorial Calendar: A carefully crafted chronology of content, painting the vibrant canvas of themes and topics.

Editorial Use: The use of an image in a context that relates to events that are newsworthy or of public interest, such as in newspapers, magazines, and educational articles.

Electronic: Images used in electronic or digital media like television or the internet. For example, online commercials or digital billboards.

EQ: Equipment. Refers to tools, machines, or other devices used in production.

Europe: Usage allowed anywhere across Europe. For example, a European hotel chain using the same images in their hotels in France, Spain, the UK, etc.

Exclusive: Only one client can use the photos. For example, a clothing brand buying exclusive rights to photos shot by a professional.

Exclusive Rights: A licensing agreement where the image is sold to one user, and no one else can buy or use that image for the duration of the agreement.

Exclusive to Industry: Usage is exclusive within a certain industry. For example, a car manufacturer ensures that their car photos aren't used by other automakers.

Exclusivity: Degree to which the usage of the photographs is restricted to a single user or a specific set of users.

Fair Use: A legal principle that permits limited use of copyrighted materials without needing permission from the rights holders. It applies mainly in scenarios like commentary, criticism, news reporting, or academic research.

First Ownership: In the majority of cases, the photographer will be the first owner of the copyright of a photograph.

FOB: Front of book. Initial pages of a magazine, including the table of contents, editor's note, and brief articles.

FPO: For position only. Temporarily placed in a design to indicate where the final image will be placed.

Full-Buyout: A full-buyout agreement in a photoshoot is a contractual agreement in which the client pays a one-time fee to obtain complete ownership and control of the images captured during the shoot. This type of agreement grants the client unlimited and unrestricted use of the images for all purposes, without needing to seek permission or pay additional fees to the photographer in the future.

Geographical Region: The specified locations where the use of photographs is permitted.

Global/International: Usage allowed anywhere in the world. For example, McDonald's uses the same images across all its global branches.

HMUA: Acronym for hair and makeup artist.

Infringement: Unauthorized use of copyrighted work, such as using an image without permission or appropriate licensing, which violates one or more of the copyright owner's exclusive rights.

Internet: Images specifically used on the internet. For example, a business using images on its website or on its social media platforms.

Invoice: A document sent to clients that details the services provided, the cost of those services, and payment terms. Invoices are essential for tracking income and ensuring timely payment from clients.

Key Art: The primary artwork used to promote a creative visual property such as a film or video game.

KO: Kick off. To start or begin something.

Layout: The creative choreography of text and visuals dancing seamlessly across the pages.

Licensing: The process of granting permission for someone else to use your photographs, often in exchange for a fee. Licensing your images can be a valuable source of income for freelance photographers.

Limited: Rights of usage that come with certain restrictions, usually related to time, scope, or media. For example, for a single event or just for digital media.

Local: Use confined to a specific local area/city. For example, use of photos in a local newspaper.

Magazine: Images used within a magazine. For example, editorial or advertising photographs in a lifestyle magazine.

Market: The target audience for whom the photographs are intended.

Marketing: The process of promoting your photography services to attract new clients and generate business. Marketing strategies can include social media, email campaigns, networking, and advertising.

Masthead: The emblem of a publication's identity, a beacon that declares, "Here we stand!"

Media: The platform or medium of use for photographs.

Metadata: Metadata is information that provides additional details about a specific piece of data. It gives context and describes various aspects of the data, making it easier to understand, organize, and retrieve.

Model Release: A legal release signed by the subject of a photograph granting permission to publish the photograph in one form or another. The necessity of a model release depends on the intended use of the photograph.

Mood Board: A collection of images, colors, textures, and other visual elements used to convey the visual style and direction of a commercial shoot.

National: Usage only within one specific country. For example, images used by a national retailer in the USA.

Networking: The process of building relationships with other professionals and potential clients in the photography industry. Networking can lead to referrals, collaborations, and new business opportunities.

Newspaper: Images used in newspapers specifically. For example, a photo accompanying a news article.

Non-Exclusive: Multiple clients may use the photos simultaneously. For example, a stock photo used by various businesses in their marketing materials.

Non-Exclusive Rights: A licensing option that allows multiple parties to license and use the same image simultaneously. It contrasts with exclusive rights, where only one person or entity can use the image.

North America: Usage across the countries in North America. For example, a North American food chain using images in their branches in the USA and Canada.

Out-of-Home (OOH) or Outdoor: Images used in advertising mediums that reach the consumers while they are outside their homes. For example, billboard or transit advertisements.

PA: Production assistant vs. photo assistant. Both roles support the main photographer or director; the production assistant often deals more with administrative, organizational, or physical tasks, whereas the photo assistant actively assists on photoshoots.

Plates: Individual portions of a photoshoot or layers of an image intended to be combined in post-production.

Point-of-Sale (POS) or Point-of-Purchase (POP): Images used in advertising placed around merchandise. For example, in-store signage or product packaging.

Portfolio: A curated collection of your best photographic work, showcasing your skills, style, and range as a photographer. A strong portfolio is essential for attracting clients and securing photography jobs.

Pricing: The process of determining how much to charge for your photography services. Pricing should take into account factors such as your skill level, expenses, and the market in which you operate.

Promotional: Images used to boost brand recognition or to generate interest in a product. For example, in a marketing brochure or on social media.

Property Release: A legal release signed by the owner of the property used in a photograph (e.g., a building, pet, or artwork) that grants permission to use or publish the photograph.

Proposal: Written documents that outline the details of a photography project, including the scope of work, timelines, and pricing. Proposals are often used to secure photography jobs with clients.

Public Domain (PD): Creative works not protected by intellectual property laws, such as copyright, trademark, or patent laws. These works may be used freely without the permission of the former copyright owner.

Public Performance Rights (PPR): The legal rights to publicly show a copyrighted work, like an image in an exhibition.

Public Relations: Images used to shape public perception of a person, organization, or event. For example, press release photos or event images for a charity event.

Regional: Use in a specific larger region, like the Midwest or Southeast Asia. For example, images used in marketing to a specific regional customer base, like photos of clothes on a Southeast Asian e-commerce platform.

Release Form: A legal document signed by the subject of a photograph, granting permission to publish the photograph in one form or another.

Reputation: The perception of your photography business by others, including clients, peers, and the general public. A positive reputation can lead to more business opportunities and long-term success.

Reuse: The act of utilizing the same photographs for different purposes or occasions. For example, a retail store reusing holiday-themed photos for consecutive holiday seasons.

RFP: Request for proposal. A document sent to potential vendors, inviting them to submit a proposal for a product or service needed by the business.

Rights Managed (RM): A type of image license that allows the one-time use of the photo as specified by the license. If the user wants to use the photo for other uses, an additional license needs to be purchased.

Rights/Quantity: The legal and factual allowance for using the photos. The quantity references the number of times a photo can be used. For example, usage in two different ad campaigns.

Royalties: Payments made to photographers for the ongoing use of their images, typically as a percentage of sales or a fixed fee per use. Royalties can be a source of passive income for freelance photographers.

Royalty-Free (RF): A type of image license that involves the user paying a one-time fee to use the photograph multiple times for multiple purposes, without paying additional royalties.

SEO: Search engine optimization. The process of maximizing the number of visitors to a particular website by ensuring the site appears high on the list of results returned by a search engine.

Shot List: A document that maps out what will happen and who will be on camera during every shot of a film or video.

SOW: Scope of work. The specific tasks, services, and deliverables that the photographer will provide.

Stock Photography: Ready-to-use photographs that are licensed for specific uses. They are often used to fulfill the needs of creative assignments instead of hiring a photographer.

Style Guide: The compass that guides our unified voice, ensuring our message is clear, coherent, and filled with vibrancy.

Time Period/Length of Time: The predefined time frame during which the photographs can be used. For example, a six-month campaign.

TK: To come. A term used in the publishing industry to indicate something that will be added later.

TOC: Table of contents. An ordered list of the parts of a book or document organized in the order in which the parts appear.

Total Buyout: Full rights are bought by the client, providing them with sole ownership and unlimited usage of the photographs as desired. For example, a stock photo company buying rights to an image to resell.

Trade: Images aimed at professionals or other businesses. For example, a manufacturer using a photo in a business-to-business catalog.

Trade Show: Images used in a trade show context, usually for promotional purposes. For example, on banners or merchandise at a booth.

Unlimited: Here, the client has unrestricted use of the photographs without time, geographic, or media limits. For example, the photos can be used indefinitely, in any media and any location.

Usage Realm: The environment or context in which the photographs are utilized.

Verticals: Specific topic areas or specialized segments within a broader market or industry.

Watermark: A visible or invisible mark added to a photograph to protect against unauthorized use and identify the copyright owner. Watermarks can be a simple text overlay or a more complex logo design.

WIP: Work in progress. An unfinished project that is still being added to or developed.

Work for Hire: A work created by an employee as part of employment or a work commissioned under certain circumstances, where the copyright is owned by the employer or person who commissioned the work, not the creator.

Wrap: The process of finishing a shoot, including dismantling and packing up equipment, cleaning the location, and notifying all relevant parties that the production has concluded. "Wrap" can also be called out by the director or another authority figure to signify the end of the shoot.

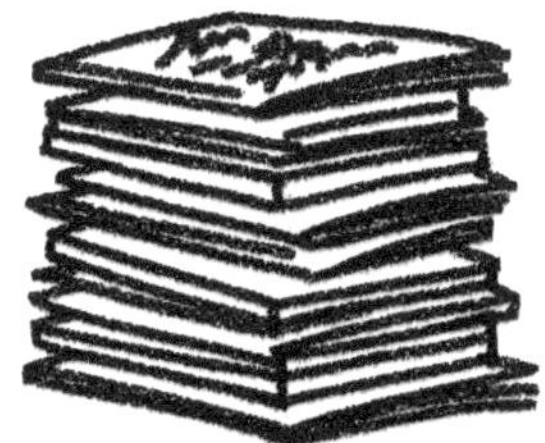

NOTES

[1] "Biography: The Gordon Parks Foundation," The Gordon Parks Foundation, Accessed August 14, 2024, gordonparksfoundation.org/gordon-parks/biography

[2] David Marchese, "Jann Wenner Defends His Legacy, and His Generation's." The New York Times, Published September 15, 2023, nytimes.com/2023/09/15/arts/jann-wenner-the-masters-interview.html

[3] Frankel, David. 2006. The Devil Wears Prada. United States: Fox 2000 Pictures.

[4] *"What Is the Role of Each Member of the Editorial Team?,"* Trade Association Business Publications International, Accessed December 16, 2024, tabpi.org/faq/what-is-the-role-of-each-member-of-the-editorial-team

[5] *"What Is the Role of Each Member of the Editorial Team?,"* Trade Association Business Publications International, Accessed December 16, 2024, tabpi.org/faq/what-is-the-role-of-each-member-of-the-editorial-team

[6] *"What Is the Role of Each Member of the Editorial Team?,"* Trade Association Business Publications International, Accessed December 16, 2024, tabpi.org/faq/what-is-the-role-of-each-member-of-the-editorial-team

[7] patsydesign2014. "Roles of Magazine Editorial/Design Team." Patricia Gomez, Published January 28, 2015, patriciasdesignsite.wordpress.com/2015/01/28/roles-of-magazine-editorialdesign-team

[8] patsydesign2014. "Roles of Magazine Editorial/Design Team." Patricia Gomez, Published January 28, 2015, patriciasdesignsite.wordpress.com/2015/01/28/roles-of-magazine-editorialdesign-team

[9] "Layout Artist." Edmates, March 7, 2024, edmates.com/career-guide/layout-artist

[10] Kaplan Community Career Center. "What Does an Interactive Designer Do? Career Overview, Roles, Jobs | KAPLAN," Accessed December 16, 2024, jobs.community.kaplan.com/career/interactive-designer

[11] "Photo Researcher | Encyclopedia.com," Accessed December 16, 2024, encyclopedia.com/economics/news-and-education-magazines/photo-researcher

[12] "How to Become A Digital Editor | Indeed.com," Published July 15, 2024, indeed.com/career-advice/finding-a-job/how-to-become-digital-editor

[13] Ed Heil, "What Is a Video Producer and What Do They Actually Do?," Storytellervideos.com (blog), Published July 14, 2024, Accessed December 16, 2024, storytellervideos.com/blog/video-producer

[14] Staff, Coursera. "What's a Social Media Manager? And How to Become One." Coursera, Published November 18, 2024, coursera.org/articles/how-to-become-a-social-media-manager

15 "Nondisclosure Agreement." In *Merriam-Webster Dictionary*, Accessed October 4, 2024, merriam-webster.com/dictionary/nondisclosure%20agreement

16 "Estimate." In *Merriam-Webster Dictionary*, Accessed October 5, 2024, merriam-webster.com/dictionary/estimate

17 "What Is Cinematography and What Does a Cinematographer Do?," American Film Institute, Accessed December 16, 2024, afi.com/news/what-is-cinematography-and-what-does-a-cinematographer-do

18 Indeed Editorial Team. "What Does A Content Creator Do?" Indeed.com, Updated July 31, 2023, indeed.com/career-advice/finding-a-job/content-creater

19 Zip Recruiter Marketplace Research Team. "What is a Digital Imaging Specialist and How to Become One," Accessed December 16, 2024, ziprecruiter.com/career/Digital-Imaging-Specialist/What-Is-How-to-Become

20 Jen Warren, "Crew: What DigiTechs Do." Wonderful Machine, Published February 4, 2021, wonderfulmachine.com/article/crew-digitech

21 Jirsa, Pye. "5 Responsibilities of a Photography Lighting Assistant." SLR Lounge, Updated November 16, 2024, slrlounge.com/5-responsibilities-of-photography-lighting-assistants

22 Bock-Schroeder, Jans. "The Art of Photo Curating," Updated October 28, 2022, bock-schroeder.com/photo-curator

23 Kaplan Community Career Center. "What Does an Image Archivist Do? Career Overview, Roles, Jobs | KAPLAN," Accessed December 16, 2024, jobs.community.kaplan.com/career/image-archivist

24 Paul, Leah. "What Does a Photo Editor Do?" Mediabistro, Published December 13, 2016, mediabistro.com/climb-the-ladder/skills-expertise/what-does-photo-editor-do

25 Salary.com. "Photography Studio Manager Job Description | Salary.com," Accessed December 16, 2024, salary.com/research/job-description/benchmark/photography-studio-manager-job-description

ACKNOWLEDGMENTS

I would like to express my deepest gratitude to the incredible Krista Dunbar. You took my ramblings and words and made my thoughts and ideas into a beautiful book. Thank you to Tina Dupuy, without whom this book would not exist. Thank you to Liz Morrow and Ashton Renshaw for helping me create an amazing book proposal. Thanks to Natalia Price-Cabrera and Natalie Potell, who helped edit this book. Thank you to my amazing designer and illustrator, Michelle Clement—you brought my vision to life.

I'm also incredibly thankful for the love and support of my family—my mom, my dad, and my sister—as well as the unwavering belief and encouragement of Brenna Chambliss, Libby Micheletti, Kelly Frush, and Ava La Vida Coaching. Thank you to Gabriela Hasbun and Yasmina Mattison, the amazing cover photographer and cover model.

Thank you to all the people who have been with me through all the ups and downs on the journey of the publishing of this book. I wouldn't be here without you all. Lastly, I am humbled and grateful for the guidance and inspiration bestowed upon me by God, who gifts me with the spirit of love and courage.

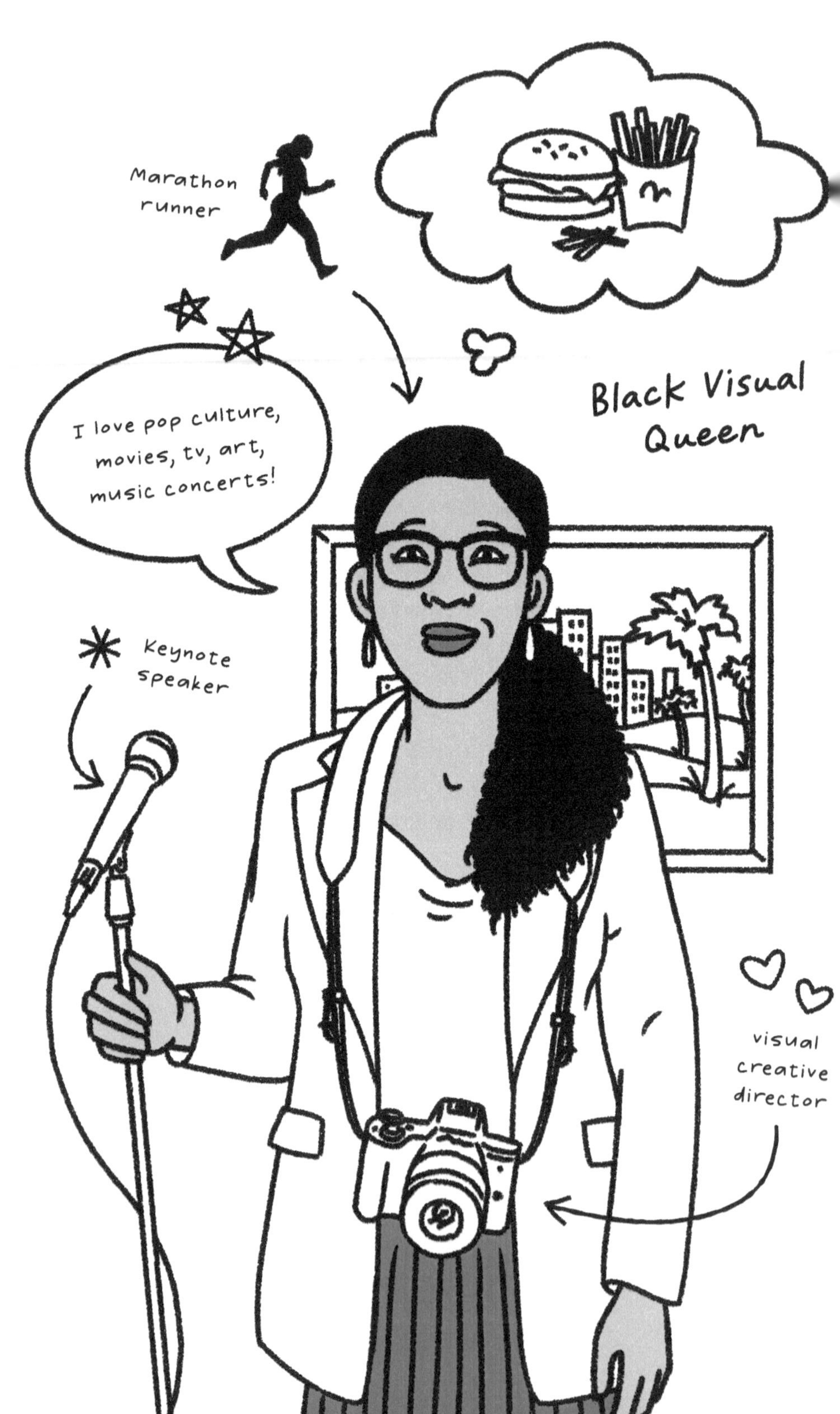
Marathon runner
I love pop culture, movies, tv, art, music concerts!
Keynote speaker
Black Visual Queen
visual creative director

ABOUT KAREN

I'm passionate about mentoring and coaching the next generation of aspiring photographers in the brand and editorial industry. With over ten years of experience as an industry insider, I believe in providing equal access to information and am dedicated to being a resource for others. As a visual creative director, keynote speaker, and founder of the photography coaching firm Black Visual Queen, I've had the privilege of working with iconic brands and editorial publications. In my free time, I love training for marathons and diving headfirst into all things pop culture.

BLACK
VISUAL
QUEEN ®

www.ingramcontent.com/pod-product-compliance
Lightning Source LLC
Chambersburg PA
CBHW021532150726
47990CB00006B/2199